R.E.S.E.T. YOUR *Mindset*

R.E.S.E.T. YOUR *Mindset*

NATALIE ECKDAHL, MBA

R.E.S.E.T. Your Mindset
Non Fiction

Text copyright 2018 by Natalie Eckdahl

Cover designed by Seedlings Online at www.seedlingsonline.com
Ebook productions by E-books Done Right at www.ebooksdoneright.com
Paperback formatting by Atthis Arts at www.atthisarts.com

All rights reserved. Except as permitted under the US Copyright Act of 1976, no part of this publication may be reproduced, stored in a retrieval system, or transmitted in any form or by any means electronic, mechanical, photocopying, recording, or otherwise, without written permission of the author. For information regarding permission, send a query to the author at natalie@bizchix.com

Every effort has been made to ensure that the content provided herein is accurate, up-to-date, and helpful to the reader at the time of this publishing. However, this is not intended to replace or treat any conditions, nor is it an exhaustive treatment of the subject. We encourage anyone to seek help with a professional counselor, therapist, or doctor where issues deem it necessary. No liability is assumed. The reader is considered responsible for your choices, actions, and results undertaken after reading this work.

Visit www.bizchix.com for more information about the author, updates, or new books.

ISBN

978-1-946508-17-1 (paperback)

978-1-946508-18-8 (ebook)

Table of Contents

DEDICATION
ACKNOWLEDGMENTS

R.E.S.E.T. *Framework*

1. HEALING FROM THE STAGE 3
   Rock Bottom
   Desire vs. Fear
   Come Back Again

2. THE R.E.S.E.T. FRAMEWORK 9
   Mindset is Not One and Done
   Let's R.E.S.E.T.
   R — Recognize
   E — Evaluate
   S — Story
   E — Enough
   T — Take Action
   R.E.S.E.T Again

3. EVERYONE'S A MESS 19
   The Struggle is Real
   Stop Comparing
   Comparing Outsides to Our Insides

4. SILENCE YOUR INNER MEAN GIRL 23
   Research on Self-Talk
   Effects of Our Childhood
   The ACE Study
   Nature vs. Nurture
   The Limits of Success
   Unintentional Shame
   The Stories We Tell Ourselves
   Transforming your Self-Talk
   The New You

Mindset Battles

5. **IMPOSTER SYNDROME** 35
   - What Is It?
   - Imposter Syndrome on a Celebrity Level
   - Diving Deeper
   - Meet Danielle Liss
   - You Are Not Alone
   - Owning Your Own Expertise
   - Working Through It

6. **FEAR OF FAILURE** 44
   - Perfectionism
   - My Perfectionism Story
   - Ship It
   - Comparisons
   - You Will Fail
   - Take It from Them
   - How to Get Through Perfectionism

7. **FEAR OF SUCCESS** 53
   - What is Fear of Success?
   - How Do I Know?
   - You Are In Control
   - Meet Karen DeYoung
   - Coping with Success
   - Couple Success with Failure

8. **FEAR OF JUDGMENT** 60
   - Judging Others
   - Self-Judgment
   - Judgment from Your Friends and Family
   - Judgment from Your Community
   - Judgment from Your Industry
   - PMS
   - Six Quick Tips

9. **LIMITING BELIEFS** 68
   - VIP Days
   - The Law of Averages
   - The Power of Competition
   - Others' Limiting Beliefs
   - They Won't Pay That Much
   - The Inner Mean Girls Scripts
   - Actual Limiting Beliefs
   - Silencing Strategies

10. **MONEY MINDSET** 78
    My Money Mindset Story
    Abandonment
    Scarcity—Meet Jacqueline Snyder
    Dealing with Scarcity
    Meet Betsy Furler—Getting Help with Your Numbers
    Our Own Ceilings
    Labels
    Both/And Instead of Either/Or
    Can't Take Money
    You Can't Sell Here
    Your Belief Systems about Money
    Reframing
    Respect Money
    Working Hard and Self-Worth
    One Final Thought

Take Action Solutions

11. **TAKE IMMEDIATE ACTION** 97
    What's Next?
    Ways to Take Action
    How to Take Action
    5, 4, 3, 2, 1 it!

12. **SELF-CARE** 105
    What is Self-Care?
    Men vs. Women
    Where to Start
    Self-Protection
    What You See May Not Be Real
    A Few More

13. **AFFIRMATIONS** 115
    The Power of Positivity
    Meet Tara
    Creating Opportunities
    Make Them Work
    Eight Quick Tips to Get Started
    List of Affirmations

14. VISUALIZATION 122
    The Power of Seeing It in Your Mind
    Visualization in Action
    Psychocybernetics
    The Reticular Activating System
    More Votes for Visualization

15. GRATITUDE 128
    Wanting What You Have
    Love Your Business
    Celebrating Your Wins
    Skewing Negative
    Meditation
    How to Get Started

16. GROWTH MINDSET 134
    Meet Amber Hawley
    Growth vs. Fixed Mindset
    Childhood Mindsets
    Changing Your Mindset
    For Those in a Dark Place
    Resiliency
    You Are Here

17. R.E.S.E.T. AGAIN AND AGAIN 140

    ABOUT THE AUTHOR 143
    REFERENCES 145

Dedication

This book is dedicated to my VIP's.

Mark, you are my rock, biggest cheerleader, and best advisor. Thank you for all the sacrifices you've made to help me build BizChix and for the time to write this book.

Aurora, you are an incredible human on all levels and I am amazed by your mind, your diligence, your focus and your courage. I don't just love you, I like you too.

Tahoe, you make friends everywhere you go and I love how you can see the big picture. You are kind, empathetic and generous.

Jett, you have the best laugh and the strongest will which I know you will keep us young and on our toes! You are charismatic, persuasive and fast (living up to your name).

Dad, you showed me that being an entrepreneur was worth it and I will never forget you showing up for 3:00 pm volleyball games and swim meets when other dad's were at their J.O.B.

And last, but certainly not least, Mom, you taught me that I could do anything I set my mind to and I believed you! What a gift. You are my best friend.

I love you all!

Acknowledgments

Writing my first book was a much bigger endeavor than I imagined. I even had mindset issues around writing a mindset book! Hello imposter syndrome! I had to smack that one down more times than I care to count.

First, I must thank the women who generously and courageously shared their personal mindset stories, Amber Hawley, Betsy Furler, Danielle Liss, Dr. Goldi Jacques-Maynes, Jacqueline Dadon Snyder, Karen DeYoung, Shannon Crow, and Tara Humphrey. Your willingness to share your experiences will help women around the globe not feel alone.

To my clients, past and present, working with you has shaped my understanding of mindset. Without your vulnerability in our sessions, sharing what goes on inside your head, and revealing what holds you back, I would not have the depth and breadth of understanding of this subject.

To my team, especially Shelli Warren and Tiffanie Jordan, who encourage, empower and support me to reach more women.

To my family, for allowing me time to write even when we were on vacation.

For my writing coach Katie Cross, thank you for the accountability, support, encouragement and more.

For the entire book team, thank you for lending your genius to the cover, layout, and edits.

To the global BizChix community, thank you for being so encouraging of my work. You inspire me every day with your courage to start and run businesses that are changing the world and supporting your families. I would not have written this book if it wasn't for you. You give me a significance in this world I never dreamed possible. Thank you.

For exclusive access to all the interviews with the high-performing women featured in this book and companion worksheets to help you on your mindset journey, visit www.bizchix.com/RESET.

R.E.S.E.T. YOUR *Mindset*

R.E.S.E.T. Framework

RECOGNIZE

EVALUATE

STORY

ENOUGH

TAKE ACTION

R.E.S.E.T YOUR MINDSET

Copyright ©2018 by Natalie Eckdahl

Chapter 1
Healing From the Stage

> "A gem cannot be polished without friction, nor a man perfected without trials."
> —*Lucius Annaeus Seneca, Roman philosopher and Statesman*

I. AM. BACK.

In October 2017, I stood on a stage with a crowd of high-powered female entrepreneurs staring at me.

A million thoughts spun through my head. Women from five countries and twenty-two states had flown to Southern California to attend a three-day conference hosted by me. These women knew me through my podcast which I launched three years before from my master bedroom closet with no audience and no broadcasting experience.

I had built a global community from nothing and now they were in front of me giving me a standing ovation. I could feel their love. They were proud of me.

The one thought that kept coming to me was this:

The old me is back.

The me that had been crushed fourteen years before. The me I had been trying to get back to, but kept only getting 90% of the way there. The me that was the woman I knew I could be—no, was *meant* to be. That moment under the lights culminated the end of my first live event.

BizChix Live was the biggest thing I'd ever attempted and the biggest financial and professional risk I've ever taken. "This was the best event I've ever attended," participants said afterwards.

"Thank you for taking such great care of us."

"You are amazing."

"Thank you for creating this."

I was blown away. The result I dreamed about turned out better than I'd imagined! But most of them didn't know my whole story. They didn't know the mindset issues I had struggled through to get there.

Starting at the bottom has a way of giving a lot of perspective.

Rock Bottom

Fourteen years ago, I lay alone on my kitchen floor in a crumpled ball, ugly crying and not sure when I would stop. That moment launched a year that I barely remember, except for wisps of deep depression and crippling anxiety.

My husband, my high school sweetheart, the man I had put through law school and who had put me through graduate business school. The father of our one-year-old daughter had cheated on me with his coworker for the last five months. A woman that I knew and who knew me. To make it even worse...

Everyone in his law firm knew.

Soon, our family and friends would know too. The affair was already public, so there was no way to keep it private and mourn in silence. It was overwhelming to even go out anywhere. It seemed as if everyone in my world somehow knew. I could feel people talking about me when I wasn't there. Or maybe when I was.

The day that I found out, a piece of me was lost. Many pieces, actually. Betrayal at that level knocked the ground out from beneath me. No matter who you are, that kind of revelation will wipe you out, at least for a season. Maybe a few years.

My daughter was a year old when I found out about his infidelity. The next four-and-a-half years were a rollercoaster of many attempts to make the marriage work. Unfortunately, it didn't survive. But I did! I settled into my new normal as a single mom, a role I had never anticipated.

Along the way, I decided I didn't like wearing the coat of victimhood, so I worked hard. I grew as a woman. I took back those things that had been taken from me—like my very identity—but a small part had still been missing. It had been missing for a long time.

What does all this have to do with mindset?

Everything.

In order to recover and heal, I have had to do deep work on myself and use every tool available to improve my confidence and paint a new future for myself and my daughter.

This therapy and mindset work has helped me in my own business and allowed me to help the women I have the privilege of coaching.

You see, there's a battle going on inside your head that highly impacts you as an entrepreneur. The thing about this war? We're battling ourselves and the way we talk about ourselves. It stops us from going to the next level or launching the next thing. It's paralyzing to think, I can't do this next step. I just can't.

The good news is that you *can* do that next thing. You can. You have the power and ability to make it happen, whatever it is.

Again and again.

Desire vs. Fear

The difficulty in being a female entrepreneur and CEO of a company is that we battle—and desire—a lot of things. After working with hundreds of women one-on-one and in group mastermind settings, I can tell you what I see. Women have a push/pull relationship between what they desire and their fears. Perhaps you relate to some of these statements.

- You want to put yourself out there as a thought leader, but you are scared you won't be accepted.
- You want a flexible schedule, but you don't have good boundaries with your clients.
- You want financial security, but your worry you'll lose clients if you raise your prices.
- You want to connect deeper with others like you, but you don't make the time to get out and meet people.

Our desires and our fears don't have to be at war. We don't have to sacrifice what we want because of the fears we face. And if you think you do, you're holding a limiting belief. We'll talk more about that in Chapter Nine.

We all have personal battles going on in our mind. Many women I work with have been through far worse than I have. As their coach, I've heard their intimate stories—sometimes things they've never told anyone else before. They've battled the loss of a child, abusive parents, severe poverty, alcoholic partners, addiction, living in foster care, molestation, rape, eating disorders, and more.

Not only are these situations emotionally, spiritually, and physically difficult to survive, but they spawn mindset issues that hold us back. We believe, *I'm not good enough*, or *I could never do that*, or *who am I to do this big thing?* We believe we're frauds. Imposters. Not meant for dreams bigger than us.

In order to become the woman, business owner, and leader you are meant to be, you have to face these mindset issues and be brave enough to battle for your desires.

That's why you're here.

I have the tools and strategies and mindset hacks to help you work through what you're experiencing. Together, we'll slash through those limiting beliefs. We'll stop self-sabotage. We'll show you that no, you're not a fraud or an imposter. You're a powerful woman, and you can do it.

When it comes to things like mindset, some days are harder than others. There are days when you feel like you just can't do it. Like when you compare the inside of your business—and your life—to the outside of someone else's by surfing all those social media posts from seemingly perfect people that have their own mindset battles.

Let's get real. They aren't perfect.

I know what it's like to struggle with not feeling good enough. To feel the pressure of single parenthood. Of teenagers. Of working with newborns and young kids. To deal with marriage issues. Or money mindset issues. Or limiting beliefs. Or tight time margins where it seems you'll *never* get it all done.

I've been there.

Honestly, I'm a mess. And let's be real—you are too.

I hope that hearing my story and the stories of other women in this book will help you, especially on those days when you're not feeling as strong. No matter where you've come from or what you've been through, you can reach your dreams. You can make your big goals come to life.

I believe that for you.

Dream it. Do it.

Come Back Again

It's important for you to know that mindset issues aren't simple.

You can have any of the mindset issues that we're going to discuss alone, or in combination, or all of them at once, like a perfect storm.

Many of them you'll cycle through again and again. Any mindset issue can be crippling—and sometimes we don't even realize that's what holding us back—but oftentimes we're battling more than one.

R.E.S.E.T. Your Mindset can be read all the way through, but expect to come back and study the specific mindset issues you are dealing with at the time. This is a reference and a guide, not a one-and-done book. This is a resource for whenever you need it.

Because you'll need to keep coming back.

I've watched people get stuck in mindset for long stretches of time. This book can help you find the nuggets you need at the right moment to propel you a step forward. The methods in the R.E.S.E.T. Framework can get you out of your head so you aren't spinning in the same spot forever.

Just brace yourself for it. Each time you go to the next level, you'll be confronted with a mindset issue.

Every single time.

Every time you do something new (like write a book, create a new program, start a speaking engagement, become a mentor, raise your prices etc.), you'll hit a mindset issue. I liken them to a punch in the stomach that keeps coming back. That's why it's important to be here, learn these steps, and take them with you.

Let's say you realize you're experiencing Imposter Syndrome—that's a great time to come back and re-read that chapter. Not only is it helpful to get some perspective, but to read again the examples of other women that feel the same way. Experiencing a lot of judgment? Come back and visit the chapter on how to deal with judgment. This book is an excellent resource for *anyone* that's constantly facing mindset issues because I know the R.E.S.E.T. Framework actually works.

One caveat here—if you feel you're dealing with a mental health issue, it's really important to talk to a professional.

I have personally dealt with anxiety and situational depression and have needed to seek out help therapists, psychologists and medical doctors. It has been a very powerful experience to receive this help and has made me a better wife, mother and coach. This book will not provide the full spectrum of help you need if you're dealing with a mental health issue. That needs to be treated first—or in conjunction with—a qualified professional.

Listen, the world needs the best you. We are growing businesses that are impacting the world and creating jobs for others. Mindset work is not easy but it is rewarding. On the other side is a client that needs you. Growth in your business allows you to grow your team and/or provide for your family's future. I am so proud of you for leaning into this. You are amazing and I believe in you!

Chapter 2
The R.E.S.E.T. Framework

> *"Transformation is a process, and as life happens, there are tons of ups and downs. It's a journey of discovery—there are moments on mountaintops and moments in deep valleys of despair."*
>
> —*Rick Warren, author and pastor.*

Coaching female entrepreneurs has given me a unique insight and perspective into what mindset issues women face and how to most effectively deal with them. I have learned that mindset isn't conquered, but it can be reset.

Mindset is Not One and Done

First of all, let's get one thing straight: your mindset issues will not end when you finish this book. Or beat your current level of Imposter Syndrome. Or release the hidden secrets of your past that are holding you back.

Mindset issues will keep coming back.

Mindset is a process.

Most of my clients start with the impression that they'll deal with mindset issues once and be done. They're powerful women who are used to finding something to conquer ... and then they conquer it. Unfortunately, mindset issues are not something that you can conquer, but you can reset them. If you know that up front, it won't take you by surprise.

My client, Tara Humphrey (more on her later), earned her MBA while working and raising her young family. She walks ultramarathons and runs her own successful business with a team. She *knows* how to work through difficult things. After struggling through Imposter

Syndrome, she said to me during our coaching session, "Okay, that's done. Now we will never talk about this again."

I smiled inside and said, "Okay", knowing it is not that easy. Guess what?

We did talk about it again. Many times. It was really hard for her to face the music again after having worked through it once. Tara has learned that as she grows and expands her business goals, the mindset issues resurface. The bigger the thing you want to do, the bigger the mindset struggle will be. Now, as she continues to ascend the ladder of her business from solopreneur to employer to industry leader, she still faces the ominous music of mindset issues again and again.

So will you.

The encouraging thing is that you will not stay stuck as long as you did the first time.

In this book, I'm going to teach you the process of resetting your mind as you move through your current mindset issue. When you set this book down, you'll know when you're having a mindset issue. You'll start to recognize it, then you'll know *how* to deal with it through various means of taking action. Eventually, this process becomes a normal part of your life. You'll start to work through these obstacles faster—especially as greater recognition comes.

Each time you move past a mindset issue, you move forward. It's like building a muscle, which comes in phases and with time. Your work will get better and faster. You'll get mentally stronger. When you do the next new thing, you're going to feel the mindset issues resurface again very intensely. But you'll have the R.E.S.E.T. Framework to lean on as you work through the mindset issue.

This whole process is normal.

Let's R.E.S.E.T.

After analyzing many coaching sessions and masterminds with my clients, I started to notice a pattern emerging. From this, the *R.E.S.E.T. Framework* emerged—in a convenient little acronym.

It's pieced together from thousands of hours of working through mindset issues with high-powered women entrepreneurs—many of whom agreed to share their stories in this book.

The R.E.S.E.T. Framework includes the stages you will work

through as you dig into your mindset. It includes 1) Recognize, 2) Evaluate, 3) Story, 4) Enough and 5) Take Action.

Let's get started.

R — Recognize

In the first step of the R.E.S.E.T. Framework, you recognize that something is going on that is not your norm.

Maybe you realize that you're procrastinating on something that is really important. You might be feeling a lot of anxiety when you think about moving forward. This is where you recognize that you're having a mindset issue. Initially, most people don't know what's going on!

There are two main signs that I've observed when women are struggling with a mindset issue. Use these as clues to help you recognize what's happening.

- You're not doing something you want to do. For example, you may say to yourself, *I want to write a book*, but you seem to keep putting it off. Ideas bloom through your mind, but they never make it on to the page. Maybe you've been saying for several months (or years!), *I really want to launch a podcast*, but it still hasn't happened. It could even be that you have the time and the means to do so . . . but you still don't do it.

- When you think about doing something, you feel anxiety or stress, so you don't think about it. You may have other physical symptoms, like headaches or a tightening in your chest or stomach or feeling sick or distracted or lethargic.
- You find you are self-sabotaging by missing deadlines or doing what I call "busywork" instead of the harder thing you know you should be working on.

While it may seem simple on the surface, noticing your problems is not. Are you experiencing these things now? Have you in the past? Think it over for a moment. You literally don't know what you don't know. You're totally immersed in it. Spinning in a place like that will hold you back.

Once you know that you're having a mindset issue, you've made a huge amount of progress. You can now move forward. That little piece of knowledge is really powerful. You should be very proud of yourself for getting here!

Women don't give themselves credit for the ability to see that they're having a mindset issue. The majority of people go through life without stopping to think about why they're stuck—or even realizing that they are stuck—so it *is* a big deal to recognize that you're struggling with a mindset issue.

Recognizing Without Judgment

As part of recognizing, it may be easy to think, *Ugh! I'm so stupid. I'm having a mindset issue.* Or, for those of you who've been around the block before, I often hear, *I'm having a mindset issue again! Why can't I just get this figured out?*

That is not what I want from you.

I love to draw inspiration from other specialties and areas of study, including sports psychology, clinical psychology, military leadership, business leadership, life coaches, and more. In his inspiring sports psychology book *The Inner Game of Tennis*, W. Timothy Gallway says this, "The first inner skill to be developed in the Inner Game is that of nonjudgmental awareness. When we 'unlearn' judgment, we discover, usually with some surprise, that we don't need the motivation of a reformer to change our 'bad' habits. We may simply need to be more aware. There is a more natural process of learning and performing waiting to be discovered. It is waiting to show what it can do when allowed to operate without interference from the conscious strivings of the judgmental self."[1]

Judging ourselves for something this natural will do you no favors. Mindset issues happen to everyone, which is why I want you to start looking at this step a little differently.

I love watching clients recognize they have a mindset issue. Once you recognize it, the hardest part is done.

Now we can dive right into what the mindset issue is in the next step.

E — Evaluate

This is where you evaluate what the issue is. At this stage you're probably thinking, *okay, I recognize that something is going on. What is it? What could it be?* We want to go through the possibilities and understand three things.

1. Where is this mindset issue coming from?
2. What does it mean?
3. When you're evaluating what it is, you're really discerning what the origin of your thoughts are.

Am I stuck in a belief that stems from childhood?

- Do I think I'm a fraud?
- Am I afraid of success?
- Is this Imposter Syndrome?
- Am I afraid of failing?
- Am I worried about other people judging me?
- Do I have a limiting belief?
- Am I feeling mommy guilt?
- Is this money mindset?
- Or is this the perfect storm combination of all the above?

For example, with Imposter Syndrome, I've found that knowing everyone else also feels like a fraud or fears that someone will *draw the curtain back* is helpful in itself. Understanding that you're not alone, and that Imposter Syndrome is not logical, takes some of the power out of it.

If you don't ask these questions and figure out why and what you're thinking, you'll stay in that place and never understand. The mindset issue will get worse.

At this point in my framework, I love for people to remember past successes. Looking through what you've already done—and allowing yourself to realize that you've done it—can pull you out of the downward spiral.

It's another form of evaluation that can help almost immediately.

S — Story

The next step in your mindset issue is to listen to your own self-talk. What are you saying to yourself inside your head? What story are you telling yourself? Are you creating stories for other people's behavior or response to you?

Rising Strong

I'm incredibly grateful to Brené Brown (Ph.D., LMSW) for normalizing the fact that we're telling ourselves stories that may or may not be true. It's how we're perceiving and interpreting the world—but not necessarily a reflection of the actual world.[2]

In her book, *Rising Strong,* Brown shares a story of a visit to the lake with her husband. While being vulnerable with him in an attempt to connect during a swim together, her hope for a "moment" with him didn't go the way she planned. She made up an entire story in her head about why he wasn't connecting with her. She imagined he probably thought her too overweight or old. When she asked him about it, he shared that he hadn't been thinking any of those thoughts about her, but had been worried about their safety. He was focused on watching the boats and lake traffic because of a nightmare he'd had the night before.

Which definitely wasn't the story in her head.

"Men and women who rise strong are willing and able to rumble with their stories," Brown says. "They get honest about the stories they've made up about their struggles, and they are willing to revisit, challenge, and reality-check these narratives as they dig into topics such as boundaries, shame, blame, resentment, heartbreak, generosity, and forgiveness. Rumbling with these topics and moving from our first responses to a deeper understanding of our thoughts ... gives birth to key learnings about who we are and how we engage with others."[3]

When we look at the stories we are, and have been, telling ourselves, we can sift through them to find the truth. Yes, sometimes those stories are real. Sometimes our parents are bad parents. Sometimes the limiting belief system our parents gave us was cruelly intentional—but that still doesn't make it truth.

Now it's time to ask: What story am I telling myself?

Peel back the layers of the onion a little more. You've evaluated and determined that you're experiencing some Imposter Syndrome (which typically means you're comparing yourself to someone else). Who are you comparing yourself to? Why?

With fear of failure or fear of success, you may be thinking of something a family member or mentor said in the past that's holding you back. What did they say? How is it impacting you right now?

I want you to ask: *What am I saying to myself about this mindset issue? What is my self-talk? What is my internal dialogue that creates this mindset?*

You need to get to that layer.

This is a hard step. At this point, you've identified that you have an issue, you've evaluated what it is and now you have to admit what stories you're telling yourself about it.

The What-If Protocol

You have the story that you're telling yourself about a certain thing, but it may not encompass all the what-ifs.

I find that often people don't move forward because of fear, but they haven't figured out what they would do if this big fear happened to them. I like them to *what-if* the scenario until there are no more *what-if's* available. I call this the *what-if protocol*.

Basically, I want you to get to the end of the line of this fear. Take me starting a podcast for an example. This was the progression of my what-iffing.

What if I can't get anyone to do an interview with me? What if I can't figure out the technology? What if people hate the podcast art I design? What if I record the interview, and it's terrible? What if I launch a podcast and no one listens?

Okay. End of the line. For me when I first launched my podcast, the worst thing would be no one listening. Then I sat back and asked: can I survive that?

If the answer was no, then I wouldn't have done the podcast. However, I decided that I could survive it, so I took action. Knowing that I could survive the worst-case scenario gave me the courage to figure it out.

Why does this work?

Because it forces you to face what you may not be facing. Studies have shown that because of the way the mind works, what we perceive as a risk can be distorted by our imagination.[4] What-iffing to the end can give you the strength to mentally help yourself out of procrastination and fear and create an entirely different story.

Here is the situation I had to take myself through while writing this book. I sat down and **recognized** my mindset issue, **evaluated** where it came from, found what **stories** my thoughts created around it, then I began to *what-if*. The end of the line came back to this question: what if this book totally fails?

Well, I've told my community about it already, so they'll be disappointed or think I'm a failure. I've invested money and time into it that I can't get back. I could publish it and get zero sales. Or all one-star reviews. People could call me a fraud. My pride would suffer. I may make a fool of myself.

I went there. I went to that dark place and rode down the train of *what-ifs*, and then I asked, "Can I survive that?"

Can I survive people hating the work that I love?

Can I survive judgment?

Can I survive rejection?

Can I survive loss of money?

The answer? Yes. I felt that I could survive all that. I had to get to a place where I decided that I could move on with my life even if all those horrible things happened.

I find that getting to the end of the what-ifs is usually less scary than we imagined.

E — Enough

In this step, you're going to draw a line in the sand.

You say, "I'm done."

You may be hearing this: I'm done living in this space. I'm done holding myself back. I'm done being stuck. I want this thing more than I want to stay safe. I'm done having Imposter Syndrome. I'm done being afraid that a family member will say *I told you so* if I fail. I'm done being afraid that my husband will resent me if I make more money than him.

You have to get to the point where you think, *It is more important for me to do this thing than to stay here.* Thinking through the impact here can be really helpful. Then you can look ahead and say: now I'm ready to do something.

Doesn't that feel better just reading it?

You're gaining the confidence you need to do something, but you haven't done it yet. Sometimes in this step, you may also be educating yourself on what that next step is. You've decided to move on from the mindset issue. Now is where you figure out how to do that—because you've had enough.

T — Take Action

This is the final step.

Now you do my favorite thing: you go take some action.

Take Action

Anyone who has listened to the BizChix Podcast knows that my favorite catchphrase, which I—or my two young sons—say at the end of every episode, is *go take some action*. I'm here to say yes, this is true. With mindset issues, you do need to take action. But not always right away.

Maybe, on a small scale, your action is not watching Netflix to escape. Or you might go for a walk. Call someone. Taking action with small steps can be just as powerful as big steps.

While preparing for my live event BizChix Live, I often got caught in mindset issues. They can be crippling. For me, doing something for the event, like solidifying speaker contracts or paying a vendor, helped me feel more cemented in that goal. Taking that small action was proof that I was going to make the whole goal happen. In that moment, those little actions were often enough to get me out of the rut until I could really dig deep.

One powerful step is to ask, *What is the next thing I could do on my list that moves me forward to my goal?* You could push send on your new program. Make the call you've been putting off. Decide on a new product.

Keep in mind that taking action could also be seen as caring for ourselves in the midst of the process and doing things that help us distract from inertia. We're getting ourselves out of being stuck.

Taking action is deciding not to stay in the same space anymore, which could be as simple as calling a friend or ignoring life for an hour or two. I have a whole section on taking action that will support you in Chapters 11 through 16.

R.E.S.E.T Again

I wish that once we worked through the R.E.S.E.T. Framework that we would be done. But each time you step into a new challenge from hiring to applying for an award to stepping in front of a camera to raising your prices, you will revisit your deepest fears.

But, you will get faster. Much faster. You will move learn to move through the steps with lightning speed and eventually won't even know that you are doing it.

This work on our inner selves is not easy, but it helps to know that everyone has mindset issues that they are working through.

Let's dig in by first acknowledging that everyone is a mess!

Chapter 3
Everyone's a Mess

> "Embrace the glorious mess that you are."
> —*Elizabeth Gilbert, author of Eat, Pray, Love*

I have a secret to share with you: everyone's a mess.

One of the things I do as a coach is normalize the experience of entrepreneurship. I let women know they are not alone. I'm privileged to have women share their most intimate thoughts, fears, concerns, and past histories with me. This has given me a special insight into the psyche of women entrepreneurs. I know that things aren't as pretty as they seem on your social media channels or websites. I get to see behind the scenes of hundreds of businesses and let's just say things rarely look neat and tidy under the hood. The truth is that you are a mess in some way or another. Guess what?

So am I. So are all the women you might admire or look up to or even feel competitive towards. Let's start by assessing where we are right now.

We're adults.

We're a mess.

And it's okay.

When we're kids, we never imagine that we'll be a mess. We think our dreams and plans will all work out beautifully just the way we've planned and that life will go smoothly for us. But no one has it all figured out!

I'm going to say that again.

No one has it all figured out.

The Struggle is Real

All of us have things that are harder for us to do than for others. I see women entrepreneurs struggle with these things:

- Client boundaries
- Worthiness
- Organization
- Taking risks
- Hiring
- Leading
- Conquering fears
- Technology
- Processes and systems
- Email management
- Saying no

Do any of those apply to you?

One of the best parts of my work as a coach is bringing women together in masterminds, which are small groups of entrepreneurs who meet regularly to help each other with their businesses. While there, they realize that the women they thought had it all together really don't.

And that's okay.

That is a powerful lesson to learn, which is why I'm reviewing it now. That's not the only common ground that you share with other women, either. I also know from working with hundreds of women entrepreneurs that you will identify with one, many, or all of these following statements:

- I feel like an imposter, like someone is going to discover I'm a fraud and realize that I'm not really all they think I am.
- I feel like I don't get enough done.
- I have trouble deciding on what task or project to do next.
- My email inbox is overflowing.
- My desk is a mess.
- My systems aren't fully integrated.
- My onboarding process is nonexistent.
- I feel unorganized.

R.E.S.E.T. Your Mindset

- I have recurring payments that I've been meaning to cancel for months or years.
- My receipts are at the bottom of my purse or desk drawer, or I've lost them altogether.
- I forget to eat.
- I have a difficult personal life.
- I'm scared to put myself out there.
- I feel like a mess.
- I beat myself up.
- I barely make it through my own fears.
- I have such big dreams that sometimes they scare or paralyze me.
- I don't fit in with the people around me.
- I think about my business all the time.
- My mind is often a swirling mess.
- I'm scared of success.
- I worry that others are judging me.
- I feel guilty to be a mom and a business owner because my business takes time from my family.

Welcome to the club.

Everyone is a mess, and you are normal.

Stop Comparing

Before we launch into this book about mindset, I'd like to stop something that will just create more issues.

Can we stop comparing?

Can we stop the fantasy that *the other woman* has it all figured out?

Can we stop pretending that someone else's professional photo session represents their real life?

To be honest, I'm getting tired of Instagram feeds that display only professional photos. They're beautiful, definitely, but what are we creating for ourselves when that is our level of expectation? Being aware of, and creating, the right expectations for ourselves will remove a lot of self-inflicted pressure.

So, let's review that again.

Can we stop pretending that someone else is living the dream life?

In the last year, several celebrities and highly successful people have committed suicide. From the outside, their lives seemed perfect.

Inside, they were suffering. We never know what is really going on in someone else's life, business, or mind. We only know *our* situation and *our* story. That's all we have control over anyway.

Consider this a warm-up exercise for all the goodness I have coming your way. Here are your action steps:

- **Accept that some things are messy.** Things in our business are messy, things in our life are messy, and things in our families are messy. It's normal.
- **Stop comparing your messy insides to others beautiful outsides.** Just because you *think* that someone's business looks a certain way doesn't mean it does.
- **Unfollow and unsubscribe.** You may need to unsubscribe or unfollow people that consistently make you feel less than.
- **Be grateful.** Gratitude is so powerful I've dedicated Chapter Fifteen to it. Let's think about what we *do* have instead what we *don't* have. How about this one for starters? *I am grateful that I get to do this work I love and still be a little messy.*

Comparing Outsides to Our Insides

We compare the way our business—or our life—looks on the inside to the way others look like on the outside. We do it on a personal level and a business level.

This can be as simple as looking at an Instagram post and thinking, *I could never look that good while cooking my recipes,* or *how could I ever match up to her?* Maybe you have a woman you look up to as making your ideal income, and you're certain that she has it all together.

She doesn't. None of us do.

Chapter 4
Silence your Inner Mean Girl

> "My childhood is part of my story, and it's why I'm who I am today and why my career is what it is."
> —*Misty Copeland, first African American Female Principal dancer with the American Ballet Theater*

If you do nothing more with this book other than learn to silence, or at least temporarily quiet, your Inner Mean Girl, then you will have made tremendous progress and will see transformation in all areas of your life. You see, we all have an inner dialogue constantly going on inside of our head. Most often this talk is an incredibly cruel and includes things that you would never say out loud to another human being.

There are two voices in our head that we need to identify and move forward from. After years of working through mindset issues with other women (and on my own) I have found it helpful to give your inner voice a name. For the sake of this book, we're going to call them Inner Mean Girl and Inner Kind Girl. Feel free to create your own label—maybe you want to call your Inner Mean Girl the Troll, and your Inner Kind Girl the Angel.

Whatever helps you picture them, do it.

I've had clients share with me that their Inner Mean Girl says things like:

- You are stupid.
- You are fat.
- You are lazy.
- You are worthless.
- You are slow.
- You won't succeed.
- You've failed before.

- You're ugly.
- You're not young enough.
- You're not pretty enough.
- She's better than you.
- It's not worth trying for.

Here are a few more that women business owners often hear:

- I'm not good enough.
- Who am I to think I can do that?
- How can I say I'm an expert?
- Who am I to be the leader?
- Who am I to be the boss?
- What makes me special?
- She knows so much more than I do.
- Why am I even bothering? So many other people offer this.

Throughout this book, we'll talk most about the Inner Mean Girl, especially how and when she pops up for other female entrepreneurs. But I don't want you to disregard your Inner Kind Girl. In fact, the more you ignore the Inner Mean Girl, the louder the Inner Kind Girl can speak.

Sometimes, the Inner Kind Girl is the hardest, and most rewarding, one to hear.

Research on Self-Talk

Martin Seligman is a psychologist who is best known for his work with authentic happiness—or the way we interact with ourselves. He's one of my favorites in this field because he merges science with positive change.

In a study of over 200 graduate students, Seligman and Ed Diener found that even the happiest people—the highest scoring and ranking of all—reported occasional negative moods.[5]

Do you see what that means? Even the *happiest* of people struggle with negative emotions from time to time.

So those perfect people you're following on social media? They have down days. They have crazy, hectic, pull-your-hair-out kind of moments. As we discussed earlier, even the most powerful women have days where they struggle with mindset issues.

In this, we are all the same.

In a further discussion, Seligman describes what he calls "narration" in his article *Positive psychology, positive prevention, and positive therapy*. Seligman says, "One illustrative deep strategy is "narration." I believe that telling the stories of our lives, making sense of what otherwise seems chaotic, distilling and discovering a trajectory in our lives, and viewing our lives with a sense of agency rather than victimhood are all powerfully positive (Csikszentmihalyi, 1993)."[6]

In other words—we can *narrate*, make sense of, distill, discover, and view our lives with agency. We can *choose* the stories we are narrating to ourselves and, in a positive way, change our outcomes. Instead of being victims, we can be instruments of change to create and mold the futures that we want. No matter where we have come from, there is no limit to where we can go.

We choose what we say to ourselves.

We choose what we believe.

Effects of Our Childhood

Many of the tapes you are playing in your head are the result of experiences in your past, many that go all the way back to childhood. As we peel back the layers to uncover our mindset issues and work through them, it is helpful to understand where these messages originate. Usually it is from a parent, caregiver, teacher, coach or mentor. Sometimes it is from a romantic relationship or friendship.

Once we do this we can then ask if we agree with these messages. Do we want them to still be part of our current identity?

I find that money mindset, fear of failure, fear of success and fear of judgement are deeply rooted in our childhood.

We can discuss this topic while still honoring our parents or caregivers. We aren't here to point out all the ways they failed. We're here to see the way we interpreted things as children that we're still carrying with us today. We pick up so many messages from our parents they may have never imagined or thought possible. That's okay. It's the human experience.

Please understand: if your parents were abusive in any form, I'm not pressing you to honor them. I want to acknowledge that some of you came from very abusive situations and aren't in a relationship with your parents. Some parents did unhelpful things because they didn't know there was a better approach … and then there are parents who are evil and abusive. They don't need to be honored in the same way as parents who truly did the best they could, even if it wasn't enough.

Actress Mindy Kaling said it best while discussing the Pixar hit *Inside Out* with the movie's directors. After she read the script, she said to them, "I think it's great that you guys are making a film that shows that it's difficult to grow up and that it's okay to be sad about it."[7]

Let's get started.

The ACE Study

Have you heard of the ACE study?

This revolutionary study[8] was an investigation that took place from 1995-1997 and has huge implications today. The principal investigators were Drs. Felitti and Anda, who conducted surveys of over 17,000 people.

An "ACE" (which stands for Adverse Childhood Experience) is any type of abuse, neglect, or other traumatic experience that may have happened under the age of eighteen. The results from these 17,000 people are chilling.

The ACE study showed a dramatic link between adverse childhood experiences and risky behavior, psychological issues, serious illness, and leading causes of death *as adults*. It also showed that people with higher ACE scores were likely to die up to twenty years earlier than those without.

As adults, many of us may think that we didn't have adverse childhood experiences, but keep in mind that children perceive things differently. When something is traumatic and big, it's traumatic and big no matter *what* the context is. Think about it: when you're seven, you don't have the scope of adulthood to say, *You know, in the grand scheme of things, this isn't so bad.* When we're experiencing it as small children, it *is* that bad.

> "The younger we are, the bigger the impact things that happen in our life have on us. The first five years are extremely formative."
> —Amber Hawley, MS, LMFT

Unfortunately, we take those experiences and emotions with us into adulthood.

Nature vs. Nurture

Let's start at the beginning. Of your life, I mean.

The debate over whether we're more influenced by our innate personalities (nature) versus the way we are raised and the environment we learn in (nurture) has been going since the days of Plato and Aristotle.

Recent studies show that it's not actually nature vs. nurture. It's not one or the other.

It's both.[9]

They play off each other. Carol S. Dweck, Ph.D., widely known for her revolutionary book *Mindset* says, "Today most experts agree that it's not either-or. It's not nature *or* nurture, genes *or* environment. From conception on, there's a constant give-and-take between the two."[10]

Why do I bring this up?

I think it's important to note that our natures aren't inherently "flawed" to the point where we can't change or become better, just as we all come from different environments and can still struggle with the same issues.

Our parents don't get all the blame here.

It's not just their bad genetics or the possibly difficult environment they gave us. It's not just the way you were raised. It's not just dependent on personality. It's a combination of a lot of little things that play together to affect you as an adult today.

You're not broken from the beginning.

Your parents probably did the best they could.

Mindset knows no genetic or situational bounds.

It can all be reset.

The Limits of Success

Now that we've established how important our childhood is to our current business, let's talk about different kinds of childhoods—and their impact on female entrepreneurs—I have seen in my coaching practice.

In some families, only a certain level of success is okay.

People at a high level of success may actually be criticized or vilified for their achievements. One of my clients told me about her father who used to take them on a Sunday drive every week. They'd drive around the city and eventually end up on a hill on the rich side of town. He'd point to a luxurious, sprawling mansion owned by a local dentist and say, "You see that house? He has that house because he's gouging everyone in this town."

Many of my client's families commented on *rich people*. Identifying someone based on their income—particularly in a negative light—is extremely impactful on us once we're older. Many women I speak with have subconsciously put a ceiling on their financial success because they're afraid of becoming the *rich person* their parents made comments about.

Can we pause for a moment and reflect on the fact that many of us are creating our own glass ceilings?

I know countless women that left corporate America to have more control over their opportunities and get away from anyone else creating a glass ceiling for them. Yet, because of mindset issues, *they* are creating their own glass ceiling! They are preventing themselves from growing their business and taking themselves to their highest potential.

We need to stop getting in our own way.

In other families, wealth creates the risk of alienation.

Your family may have a certain value system that makes you believe it's *not* okay to shine bright, be successful, or achieve what you set out to do. Sometimes the belief is that money is the enemy. If you have a lot of it, you're the enemy. Getting a lot of accolades is not a good thing for women raised in this kind of household. You may have kept yourself under the radar to avoid drawing attention, or to not outshine a sibling, and now you're unintentionally keeping your business low for the same reason.

Some of my clients were raised in a home where they had to be number one, or they weren't good enough. This produces a whole range of mindset issues like perfectionism, overachieving, burnout, and never being satisfied.

Let me give you a little validation: yes, your childhood has affected your business. Yes, you probably have some deep, unconscious belief systems you're holding onto that were given to you by your parents, and you don't even know it. Yes, if you're a parent, the same thing will happen to your children, and you can't really control it. Why?

Because you can't control the way they perceive things.

But guess what?

You're here, and I can help.

Unintentional Shame

Let me tell you about Danni Hall who joined me for an on-air coaching call.†

When Danni was a child, she struggled with a hearing impairment. She had countless surgeries, hospital stays, and medical appointments with various specialists. One day, after she returned from the hospital, her Dad shoved a piece of paper under her nose and said, "Look at that, will you? That bill is ridiculous."

Oh no, young Danni thought. *I'm costing my parents so much money. My medical issues are a burden to my family.*

Fast forward several years. Danni now runs her own lice removal business helping parents of children who have lice through the Alaska Lice Clinic.‡

Not surprisingly, she's working with young children. Something inside of her is drawn to the helpless state of these kids. She's very attuned to the fact that she charges parents for what she does to help their children. As a result of her experience as a young child, guilt surfaces whenever she needs to charge these parents the full amount for helping them eradicate the lice issue.

Wonder where that came from?

Danni and I have worked on her mindset issues around taking money from parents—who are willing to pay—in order to care for their children's medical issues. Can you see the roots of that mindset issue?

A few years ago, Danni asked her father about that day when he showed her the bill. Her father was shocked that she had taken it that way. "I only meant to show you what they were charging!" he said. He simply wanted Danni to see it, to be on his side regarding the medical system and cost of healthcare, not take guilt away from it and create a belief system that told her, *I am a burden. I am not enough.*

She was no burden. She was enough.

The Stories We Tell Ourselves

Remember my client that had the Sunday drive with her father? Let's go back to her because he could have told a different story.

---

† Listen to her coaching call at www.bizchix.com/317

‡ See www.thealaskaliceclinic.com for more information on her incredible business.

Instead of speaking about how the dentist, who went through at least eight years of school after high school, worked many hours of specialty training, and ran a business that required electricity, lights, x-ray machines, special equipment, and trained staff, was gouging everyone in the town, her father could have explained it in a more positive light. (This is important for you to consider because the things we tell ourselves are very powerful. More on that later.)

Consider how this could have been reframed for my client. "Look at that beautiful house. Dr. So-and-so has worked really hard and still does today to get a beautiful home like that." Or, "If you go to school, focus on one thing, and keep going, you can have a beautiful house like that too."

Very rarely do parents gift us these negative belief systems on purpose. I firmly believe that people do the best they can with the information they have.

Let's revisit Danni. Did her father mean to give her the idea that she's not worthy of the money spent to improve her hearing?

Of course not.

Her father had feelings that he shared. Unfortunately, this ended up contributing to capping his daughter's success. Now, Danni's processing how to move through this belief system, and she's making the needed changes to stop herself from self-sabotaging.

Transforming your Self-Talk

Will you sit with me here for a moment and think of a few things you allow into your head that are incredibly cruel? If a friend were to tell you that she was hearing these things, what would you want her to hear instead?

We can replace this talk by meditating on positive thoughts. It is actually one of the most amazing ways you can "Take Action" and support resetting your mindset.

There are lots of ideas for you in Chapter Thirteen.

For now, here are a few to practice with. When you hear that Inner Mean Girl rise up, let's shut her down with a few of these thoughts instead:

- You are amazing.
- You are beautiful.

- You are healthy.
- Today will be a great day.
- Everything is going to be OK.
- Things work out for me.
- My clients love me.
- My work is helping others.
- I've got this.

The New You

As you work on improving your mindset, you will start to see how those around you are stuck in their own mindset issues. You will hear their limiting beliefs. You will watch them self sabotage.

Be careful who you are sharing your hopes, dreams and goals of your business with. Not everyone in your life will understand.

There are some of you that have parents, friends or a partner who are not going to support you. You know that already.

Stop trying to get them to do something they are not going to do.

Think of them as a faucet that is broken and you are standing there with a cup of water, wanting to get your cup filled. You are so thirsty. They really never have water for you, but maybe this time you can get just a drop of water.

Listen my friend, they are never going to give you water. You need to find another place to quench your thirst.

If you know that family or friends are not going to be supportive, stop sharing with them. Stop trying to get them to agree with your path.

Let your business success speak for itself and focus on those around you that are supportive! Focus on those who encourage your Inner Kind Girl.

Now *that* is powerful. And that is what you'll be learning in this book.

Whether you're familiar with mindset issues, have never heard of them before, or are a mentor that helps others deal with them, this book is going to dive deep into all the aspects you need to reset and help you move through mindset issues as they arise.

First, we'll learn from women like you. We'll see how they have struggled, what they've struggled with, and how they worked through the various mindset issues that frequently crop up for female entrepreneurs. After that, we'll dive into ways to take action to get you out of the mindset rut.

Let's get started.

Mindset Battles

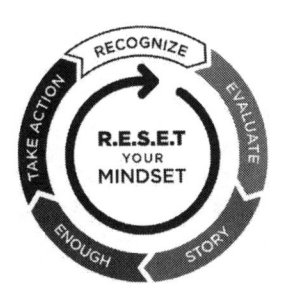

Chapter 5
Imposter Syndrome

> "I have written eleven books, but each time I think, 'Uh-oh, they're going to find out now. I've run a game on everybody, and they're going to find me out.'"
> —*Maya Angelou*

Have you ever said to yourself, "Who am I to do this?" or "I could never be as confident or successful as her," or "I feel like one day everyone is going to figure out that I have no idea what I'm doing"?

Welcome to the world of Imposter Syndrome.

The field of psychology and learning has always fascinated me, especially as it applies to women entrepreneurs. But nothing is more interesting—or, on some level, intricate—than pervasive mindset issues like Imposter Syndrome.

What Is It?

Imposter Syndrome is most easily explained by saying that you feel like an imposter in whatever world you're trying to inhabit.

It's a feeling of self-doubt, of being a fraud, or that any success has just been a fluke. When it comes to creative entrepreneurs, you may feel that sinking sense of, "I'm going to put this out there, and I have absolutely no idea what I'm talking about. Everyone is going to know."

When you're stuck in the middle of Imposter Syndrome, you never feel good enough. Some women have described it as the sensation that people are going to "draw back the curtain" and realize the truth: that you, whoever you are, are an imposter.

Is any of this sounding familiar?

I see this at all levels of success, from brand new business owners attempting to scramble together that first sale, to seasoned speakers stepping onto a new stage, to women leading seven figure businesses.

Imposter Syndrome knows no bounds. You'll find it in successful actors, CEOs, bankers, moms, athletes, politicians, educators ... and me.

Imposter Syndrome on a Celebrity Level

Sometimes we can look at celebrities and assume they have a perfect life and everything together, but they don't!

Let's hear from powerful, career-motivated women like Emma Watson, Lupita Nyong'o, and other women struggling with issues like Imposter Syndrome and discounting themselves. (Read the full article from InStyle magazine.[11])

- **Emma Watson** to *Rookie* magazine in 2013: "It's almost like the better I do, the more my feeling of inadequacy actually increases, because I'm just going, 'Any moment, someone's going to find out I'm a total fraud, and that I don't deserve any of what I've achieved.'"
- **Lupita Nyong'o:** "I go through [acute imposter syndrome] with every role. I think winning an Oscar may in fact have made it worse. Now I've achieved this, what am I going to do next? What do I strive for? Then I remember that I didn't get into acting for the accolades, I got into it for the joy of telling stories."
- **Penelope Cruz:** "I feel every time I'm making a movie, I feel like [it's] my first movie. Every time I have the same fear that I'm gonna be fired. And I'm not joking. Every movie, the first week, I always feel that they could fire me!"
- **Jennifer Lopez:** "I'm very insecure about my voice. After being told for so many years that you're not as good as this person or that person, it beats away on your insecurities ... I always wanted to be a singer and a dancer but when they start dissecting you like that, it does work away at your insecurities. You know? I'm like, 'Wow, I thought I was good at this.' It does get to you. I'm only human."
- **Padma Lakshmi:** "On the first season of *Top Chef*, I suffered from ... impostor syndrome," Lakshmi said at *Cherry Bombe's* Jubilee Conference in 2015. "I didn't have [restaurant cooking experience] ... I thought, I'll just be a really good host.

R.E.S.E.T. Your Mindset

Somewhere along there, and he probably doesn't even know it and we're friends, I heard Éric Ripert say to another chef, 'No, Padma has a really sensitive palate, like one of the most sensitive palates of anyone I've ever met.' I held on to that. Any time I felt insecure or insufficient—which I did a lot on that set—all I had to do was rely on what I did know rather than what I didn't know."

Diving Deeper

When Imposter Syndrome crops up, I know it's really a symptom of a much deeper issue. One that typically revolves around our deepest insecurities.

It sums up in the question: **who am I to do this?**

When I first started the BizChix podcast, I had a lot of Imposter Syndrome. Who was I to use podcasting as a medium to train other women? I had no radio training or journalism experience or education on how to interview other people. I recorded in my master bedroom closet. Yep. The closet. It was the only quiet space in my house at the time. After fighting in my head over it for a while, I forced myself to make an appointment to interview someone in my first episode. Why? Because then I couldn't let her down. I had someone I had to be accountable to, because I didn't think I'd do it for myself.

I did my first interview on a Saturday morning and my (new, not ex) husband and pre-teen daughter were at home. My toddler was taking his afternoon nap, and I was eight weeks pregnant with number three. My hands and voice shook as I started, but you know what?

I fought Imposter Syndrome and did it.

Here's what was going through my mind: *What if I suck at interviewing? What if no one listens? What if I embarrass myself?*

Although I didn't realize it at the time, I put the R.E.S.E.T. Framework into action.

First, I **recognized** that I felt like a podcast imposter. On **evaluating** why, I understood it was because I had almost no experience, and there was a lot that could go wrong. The **story** that I was telling myself was that I couldn't do it—but that wasn't true. So I said **enough** and decided to **take action** and do that interview.

I knew that what I wanted to accomplish—impacting women entrepreneurs and helping them grow their businesses—was bigger than the fear and self-doubt.

Meet Danielle Liss

> "I didn't know what to call it ... I didn't know I was dealing with Imposter Syndrome. I just knew that I felt I couldn't do anything ... I felt like a fraud."
> —Danielle Liss

Attorney Danielle Liss is co-owner of Hashtag Legal[†] and previous Chief Marketing Office (CMO) of a large company.

She is also intimately acquainted with Imposter Syndrome.

Let's rewind to 2016.

Danielle decided to take a huge leap in 2016 and leave her position as CMO of a large company for an influencer network to start two businesses with her friend, Jamie Lieberman. One of the businesses is Hashtag Legal. As part of this jump, Danielle set her BHAG (Big Hairy Audacious Goal)—she was going to pitch to be on a podcast she loved with a legal topic that had never been covered before.

If she could get on that podcast and talk about that thing, she would have arrived in her new world. She'd have credibility. Proof that she was someone to listen to. This was her goal. Her motivation.

Her *thing*.

While preparing dinner for her family, she turned on her podcast app to listen while working, the way she usually did. That's when she heard it.

A different lawyer, on *that* podcast, talking about *her* idea.

In that moment, she felt herself internally collapsing. To her, the culmination of her professional success had just slipped away. Danielle described it to me like this. "I felt like, *there is no room for me*. I was so fixated on that [belief] because I was so crushed. How can I make it? How can I do this?"

Shortly after that, Danielle found me.

(And spoiler alert, her virtual law firm Hashtag Legal business has grown exponentially since 2016, and they now have clients across the US.)

[†] Please visit www.hashtag-legal.com for more information. To hear her full interview (which I highly recommend!) visit www.bizchix.com/RESET

You Are Not Alone

Emily Countryman is a client of mine that runs a chain of wellness centers.† When we met, she had one location. Within two years, she scaled to five locations. By the time this goes to print, she'll probably have more. Her goal is to help men and women become healthier.

She is by far one of the most driven women that I work with. I have never heard of her not hitting one of her goals. She's at the point in her career where she has her employees run the physical store and work with the clients while she leads the team and looks for the next opportunity for the business.‡

One day while preparing to move from one location to two, she could hear her team members working with clients up front. She immediately felt like she should be out there on the front line instead of in the back, prepping for this new step.

She thought to herself, "Who are *you* to be sitting back here not doing anything? What makes you so special to be back here?"

Remember, she is the *boss*.

I asked her, "Where are you coming from with this thought?"

She didn't know. On that call, we spoke about what she was actually doing, and the way she could impact people if she grew. She couldn't work on her growth plans if she was up front, working with every single client that came in.

We weren't able to get to the base of it that day, but she did **recognize** the Imposter Syndrome issue. Some of the problem was rationalizing her role—we had to establish her goal and her why, but that wasn't the whole problem.

When she **evaluated** why she had Imposter Syndrome, she finally saw that it revolved around being the boss. The **story** she told herself was that she had to work with clients—not on the business—in order to make an impact.

Of course, she would never have been able to expand to where she is now (with five locations and more) without letting her team do the work. She had to step into the CEO role instead of being the front line team member. This is the point where she had to say **enough**.

To be honest, it took her a long time to **take action** in the office

---

† Learn more about her Washington-based business at https://idealwellnesswa.com/

‡ Emily shares this story on my podcast. Get the full epidsode here: https://bizchix.com/334

and be okay with not working directly with clients. She knew that being able to serve more men and women meant she couldn't be out front.

In the end, her desire to achieve and impact more people is what put her through this mindset issue. For a high-performing woman like her, (and all the other women I work with) overcoming Imposter Syndrome was not a quick fix.

Her desire for impact, to help more clients get healthy, to create more jobs for her community, and to ensure more financial security for her family gave her the strength to **take action** beyond the *who are you* feeling and thoughts she had in her head.

Sometimes battling Imposter Syndrome is more about stepping back and remembering priorities.

Attorney Danielle Liss was really transparent about the impetus behind her Imposter Syndrome.

"For me, Imposter Syndrome was very much about how I cope with overwhelm. It was partially trying to not get into the state of overwhelm. If I got there, it was about talking to my mastermind, my biz besties, etc. I didn't want my business partner to think I was a bad choice, or was holding her back, or wasn't worthy of being her partner."

Owning Your Own Expertise

As women scale their business and grow in all areas, they often step into their own thought leadership and become mentors.
Becoming a mentor is a breeding ground for Imposter Syndrome.

Let me give you a real life example of Imposter Syndrome in my own life. I recorded my podcast for well over a year—and 150 episodes—before I did a solo episode. Although I had people encouraging me to create solo episodes sharing my own thought leadership, I was afraid to step into my own ideas without someone else there to interview or take the attention. My audience was saying, "I want to hear *your* business trainings."

But I was thinking, *who am I to put my thoughts out there?*
Eventually, I did. Slowly.

I started off at a snail pace. First, I would write a blog post and read it out loud for the podcast. After that, it came a little easier, and I started doing it more often. Eventually, I started getting feedback. What I heard in the feedback changed the game for me—I was helping people. They

R.E.S.E.T. Your Mindset

were sending me emails saying that my trainings and encouragement, more than the people I interviewed, had impacted their life.

That is what encouraged me to do more and more on my own.

At some point in the journey I realized, *Wow! I am at the point in my career where my mentors were when they mentored me.* That was kind of weird! The tables had turned. I wasn't only a mentee now. I was a mentor as well. It was my turn to impart knowledge to others.

That's when I really did what I call *stepping into thought leadership*. I owned that I had something to share with the world and that I had a way to help women in their business.

Here's another little tidbit about becoming a mentor: it's not about age.

It's about knowledge, education, and experience. Many of my clients are older than me, but I have a level of experience in business they don't, which means they value all the things I bring to the table.

You can be a mentor if you're at least one step ahead of someone.

One other thing that enabled me to step away from Imposter Syndrome and into my own thought leadership was learning how to assess my strengths. I know now—but didn't recognize this five years ago—that I spot current trends in industries that other people don't see. I can see ahead for other people, too. I'm also intuitive and empathic. That has been very valuable to my clients and to me.

Last thing I want to cover if you're thinking about becoming a mentor: there is room for you at the table.

My client Shannon Crow also had some difficulty battling Imposter Syndrome and stepping into her own thought leadership. Shannon is a consultant for yoga teachers and runs *The Connected Yoga Teacher Podcast*[†] that helps bring visibility and attract global clients to her consultancy business while raising three kids. For her, stepping into her role within her industry had many challenges, the greatest of which was, as she explained it, feeling like there wasn't room. "I felt as if my voice wasn't needed, or there are other experts out there," she told me.

Can you relate?

So, how did she deal with that thought?

One day, when she heard another podcast like hers, she realized that the podcast she wanted to do already existed. At first, she was really disappointed. But she also knew that her messaging and experience

---

[†] Visit Shannon at https://www.theconnectedyogateacher.com/podcast/ and see her exclusive interview at www.bizchix.com/RESET

were very different. She had a different way of presenting the content and information.

Then she looked at her local situation.

"We have one hundred yoga teachers in the two counties near me, and there is enough room for all of them," she said.

To her, that meant there was room for her podcast too. And she was right! Let me reassure those of you in a similar situation. There is always room for more thought leaders.

There is always room for your voice.

Some people think, *I can't talk about this subject because there's a bigger expert talking about it.* But the way you share things will resonate with some people and not with others. In the same way, that expert you have on a pedestal resonates with some and not with others.

Secondly, sometimes experts choose to change and pivot. They may get tired. For example, Michael Stelzner, the conference founder of Social Media Marketing World, which attracts 5,000+ marketers every year to San Diego, has found that many experts in specific platforms and specific areas of thought leadership are now getting bored. They're transitioning to a completely new field or topic. In his mind, there's always room for new and fresh voices. In fact, he's searching for them.

Think about the implications there!

The "experts" may stop doing what they're doing, which would create a void. We never know what people are going to do, which is why we need to do our own thing. Each of you has a very specific style that will reach different people, a style some people are going to very much resonate with.

Shannon shared two ways to help you overcome this mental hurdle:

1. Keep telling yourself, *I just need to know one more thing than the person I'm teaching in order to be a mentor.*
2. Start off small. Shannon first led a short workshop for yoga teachers, then transitioned into a day-long workshop, then a weekend, and then an eighty-five hour certification over many weekends.

Working Through It

Let's get back to attorney Danielle Liss.

She had just heard about losing her spot on the podcast that would, in her mind, set her up as an expert. It would mean that she had "arrived" in her career.

After losing her chance, Danielle floundered. For several days, she didn't tell anyone—not her husband, not her business partner. She feared that if she said how she felt out loud, everyone would think she was crazy. Instead of reaching out, she went 100% internal and shrank away.

"Isolation was a big piece of [my response]," she said. "It was only in talking and taking myself out of the isolation that I think I was truly able to get anywhere near the root of it. It took a long time."

A side note here: like Danielle, some people are naturally more introspective than others. Some clients don't want to look back too far. Women with a lot of trauma don't want to go there or aren't ready to go there in that moment. That's okay. Do what you can to move forward even a little bit. Even a small amount of progress is better than staying stuck.

When Danielle finally reached out and talked to her friends, it was pretty simple. She told them, "I'm scared, and I'm having all these thoughts." That was enough to get the ball rolling down the right path again—even if she wasn't done.

Once she accepted there was an issue that needed to be solved, she sought out knowledge on Imposter Syndrome. She figured out her triggers—one of which was feeling overwhelmed—and experimented with ways to ease herself out of it when she could feel herself sliding into those thoughts again.

When I asked Danielle what she would tell people to do to work through Imposter Syndrome, she said, "Talk about it. If you're not ready, put it on a piece of paper. Articulate in some way what you're feeling. Don't be afraid to be a critic of the things that are in your mind."

Instead of believing the Inner Mean Girl who says, *who are you to do this thing?* I want you to start questioning back.

Who am I not to do this?

Why wouldn't there be room at the table? Heck, set another place! Add a chair. Add another leaf. Better yet, sit at another table. Ask yourself the right question instead.

Why not me?

Chapter 6
Fear of Failure

> "Courage is resistance to fear, mastery of fear,
> not absence of fear."
> *Mark Twain, author and essayist*

Being an entrepreneur takes great courage.
In the years that I've been running my business, I've spoken with hundreds of women about the fears that they face. Most of them revolve around failure—but in sneaky ways. As we walk into the fears that surround, and sometimes control, us as entrepreneurs, I feel it's important for you to see that other people have big fears too.

Here are some fears from the women I work with.

- Fear of the strength of their Imposter Syndrome.
- Fear of losing clients.
- Fear that they're concentrating on the wrong thing.
- Fear of losing respect amongst their peers.
- Fear of technology.
- Fear that their competitors are better, faster, stronger or father ahead.
- Fear of interviewing guests for a blog, podcast, or show.
- Fear that they will never be able to leave their day job.
- Fear that their efforts will fall into obscurity.
- Fear about time. Not having enough. Dividing it up between work and family. Using it well, etc.

Do you see the common thread there?
Almost all of them fear failure in some way.
None of us are immune to fear of failure. I battle my fears all the time, literally everyday. Even though I have one live event under my

R.E.S.E.T. Your Mindset

belt, I have another one coming up and the mindset issues and fear are still there.

If not bigger.

Thinking about the ramifications of all the people investing in my live event can be overwhelming and terrifying. Especially as I think about how the travel and time invested impacts their lives. They're expecting this to be great. They want to connect, learn, and work on their business.

If I were to think through that too much, I would go lay down and have a little cry. It's a lot of pressure. After a while, it gets hard to breathe. What if I fail to deliver? What if they don't feel it was worth the investment of time and resources? What if everything falls apart? What if no one shows up? What if all the attendees post on social media that they hated the event?

I'm not the only one experiencing this.

In this chapter, we're going to dive a little deeper into fearing failure, how to work through it, and steps we can take to get out of a fear-based mindset.

Perfectionism

The fear of failure is closely tied to perfectionism.

Very closely tied.

Perfectionism isn't just an entrepreneurial issue—studies link it to issues like depression[12], eating disorders[13], OCD[14], and, you guessed it, procrastination[15].

I typically see three steps with women that struggle with perfectionism: the expectation of perfection at the onset, procrastination of the work, and eventual paralysis regarding the project.

I first heard about this link a decade ago while in the audience listening to a woman speak about parenting. She said, "Perfectionism leads to procrastination, which leads to paralysis."

That hit me hard.

I realized I was missing out on the opportunity to complete something or move forward with my work because I was getting stuck in making it perfect. Procrastination was a given for me, but I didn't realize it was linked to my perfectionism.

In business, as in life, the expectation of perfection leads to procrastination. We put off something because we're expecting it to be perfect—that's a daunting task. One that, perhaps, we know from the beginning we cannot fill. Eventually, the procrastination builds until we arrive at paralysis and no work gets done.

When we expect perfection, we often end up with nothing.

When I have a client that struggles with things having to be perfect, they literally get paralyzed by their own fear of failing at the task. They get in their own head and can't move forward.

Can you imagine writing this book if it had to be perfect on the first draft or ever? You would never have it to read! The only way I can even publish it is to agree with myself to make it "good enough".

My Perfectionism Story

I am a recovering perfectionist.

In fact, I have been dealing with perfectionism since I was a child. I've had to learn, from the young age of eleven, how to manage this somewhat detrimental habit.

In sixth grade, I was getting straight A's. My teacher provided extra credit projects, and I decided to do every single one of them.

By setting such a high (and unnecessary goal), I started getting migraine headaches that became so strong I'd miss school. My mom finally took me to a doctor, who discovered that I was stressed out. I remember thinking, *how ridiculous that I'm this stressed out and am literally causing myself to get sick*. My need for perfectionism at such a young age pushed me to the point it was affecting my health and my body!

That moment taught me the powerful connection between my body, stress, and what control I had over what was happening.

Ship It

Good is good enough.

I feel like I should probably say that again.

Good is good enough.

Author Seth Godin says it best when he describes pushing your projects into the world as *shipping*.[16] "Ship often," he says. "Ship lousy stuff, but ship. Ship constantly."

For Seth, the goal is to get it out there, not to make it perfect. He says there are two places where people get stuck based on perfectionism.

1. They don't start because it has to be perfect.
2. You start, but you don't finish because—again—it has to be perfect.

Seth refers to the "lizard brain" when he speaks about fear of starting. Basically, he's talking about the amygdala—the part of our brain that's responsible for fear regulation *and fear creation*. The amygdala is where we learn to fear something that may be dangerous, but it's not a process that we control.[17] Our lizard brains act on their own, and that's good. They've kept humans alive through many very real dangers over the centuries. If something doesn't feel safe, we don't do it.

We're not fighting saber tooth tigers when we're writing an email that could get rejected, but our brain doesn't know the difference.

That's why it's so important to ship.

Practicing shipping things can be very helpful in cases like Imposter Syndrome or fear of failure. Are you holding back on providing new content because you keep tweaking the words? Are you pausing the new product line because you're afraid it's just not perfect?

Get your projects out there and get feedback!

At the very least, shipping often is getting you comfortable with submitting or posting or doing in order to get out of the insecurity and paralysis storm. If you don't ship, you never interact with your market, and you can't be successful.

For example, let's say you're creating a new course. Instead of filming hours of high definition videos and putting everything together in an expensive software, do a one-hour webinar or workshop. Charge for it to see if there's an audience that's interested. If you have takers, practice your material, and then get in front of more people.

Let's say you're writing a book. Write a short guide or a first chapter and put it out into the world. What response do you get? Who wants to read it? Why do or don't they? Will people pay for it? What format should it be in?

Take things and ship them quickly instead of waiting until you have your one big thing that's perfect and tied up in a bow.

In other words, create your minimum viable product.

Body language and lie detector expert Vanessa Van Edwards[†] was on my podcast in 2014 and illustrated this perfectly. Vanessa created

---

[†] Want to know more about the Science of People? Check Vanessa out at: https://www.scienceofpeople.com/about/

a course, infused hours of work into it, and made sure everything was exactly how she wanted it.

No one bought it. Yikes.

She learned to do a minimum viable product with everything she launches. Her husband has filmed her with her iPhone for her next projects! If a couple of people buy her product, she knows to move forward and make it bigger, better and deeper.

I love this wise approach. Not only does it help prevent the paralysis of perfectionism, but it can help curtail the paralyzing effects of Imposter Syndrome. One hundred true fans are better than people just watching.

When you expect perfection, you rob yourself of the process. The process can be very educational. And if you never ship it, you are impacting no one.

Comparisons

> "Stop comparing your beginning to someone else's middle."
> —Jon Acuff, Wall Street Journal best-selling author.

Sometimes we'll look at people who are established in their career, or their industry, and see where they are now, but not realize what it took to get there. We're not seeing the mindset issues, the roadblocks they faced, or the stops they experienced. We don't know all the things they put out into the world before the thing we're viewing now.

The problem with comparisons is that they're a trap. You can get stuck and never move forward, never put your gifts in the world, and spiral around, again and again, through fear and perfectionism.

When I was starting the podcast, I was listening to several seasoned podcasters that I admired. Instead of focusing on their newest podcasts, I went back and listened to their first ones. You know what?

They were kind of bad!

I couldn't believe how much better they were later. It made me really appreciate where they were now and that they kept the initial podcasts up. Taking them down after a few years would have made sense. When people tell me, "I'm going to go back and listen from the beginning of your podcast," I always want to say, "... ah ... maybe start at 50 or 100! Not at episode one."

But I also know the value of that early transformation. Seeing how far those other podcasters had come in just a few years gave me the confidence to move forward with my imperfect work and imperfect podcast. I hope that my early episodes give others courage to just start where they are now.

You Will Fail

This is a tricky concept to present.

Yes, entrepreneurs are famous for fearing failure. In fact, we're famous *for* failing. After Steve Jobs left Apple in 1985, they crept closer to failure with every year until their big comeback in 1997. That's twelve years of failing. FedEx kept itself alive by a narrow margin of $5,000 when it hit its lowest slump. The owners of Airbnb were printing cereal boxes to make ends meet while trying to find investors in Silicon Valley.

Failure looms over our head with every launch, every decision, and every low bank account we face. I'm not saying you should expect yourself to fail—there's no reason to have that mindset and put that out there.

But you should know that you will. At least, in some things.

As you put yourself out there and try new things, you're not going to be successful every time. It's just fact! And guess what? It's okay.

Let me normalize this for you: failure is often how business happens. In fact, failure is how business *improves*.

The first mastermind I tried to create failed. No one even signed up! Looking back, it's pretty clear why. I didn't promote it, and I didn't have a large enough audience. I was trying to launch it right before I gave birth to my son Jett, when it didn't even make sense to run a mastermind.

But I put something out there, and I learned about selling cycles, how to personally sell, and what my community really needed. Those have been invaluable lessons that have impacted my success. Guess what?

I'm glad it failed.

We don't see everyone's failures; we usually just see their successes. Basketball legend Michael Jordan lost over 350 games in his basketball career. He was often trusted with the winning shot and missed twenty-six times.[18] Thomas Edison tried 10,000 different variations of the lightbulb before he found one that worked.

Keep trying. Keep iterating. If it doesn't work, change it up. Do something different. Just keep making progress. Keep moving forward. Keep shipping.

Take It from Them

When reviewing and contemplating fear of failure, I reached out to women in my community that had struggled with it in the past, because inevitably everyone has. This is what they said about their experiences.

> **Anonymous:** "I wouldn't say I'm afraid of failure. I'm more afraid of imperfect. I'm a complete perfectionist, and much of my short time in business has been spent 'waiting until it's perfect,' which we all know is never. So, until I let go of perfect (which I'm slowly learning to do), nothing gets done."
>
> **Cathy**: "I have an area of my business that I know would help me grow, but I'm really scared of it: public relations and joint ventures. I know if I had a better visibility strategy and reached out to partner more, my list would grow so much faster. But I'm so scared to be rejected that I still haven't even started planning it."
>
> **Stacey:** "My fear of failure kept me from niching down. No matter how many times I tried to really zoom in on my ideal client, I'd broaden my language to appeal to everyone because I was afraid to make my pool of possible clients smaller."
>
> **Blair:** "I'm in the middle of [fear of failure] really with this in person workshop and mastermind. Been talking about it since February; now that we have a potential sponsor I have to be all in, and that adds an extra layer of pressure to fill seats and blow people away."

The last one I want to mention here is Goldi. You'll meet her more in-depth later. She had a fear of making decisions because they might fail. Instead of allowing herself to be overwhelmed with all the decisions and all the possible ways they could go wrong, she focused on one decision she needed to make, broke it down, and then moved into action by saying, "I'm doing this."

Often the best way to take action is to do one small thing.

No matter what you are afraid of failing at, I promise you that you're not alone.

How to Get Through Perfectionism

> "B-minus work can change people's lives. Work that you don't produce at all, does nothing in the world."
> —*Brooke Castillo, life coach.*

In the American school system, we're raised with the idea that we need to always be achieving the A. If you're the type of person that did, it can be really hard to follow through with the idea of doing anything less than perfect.

I love author and life coach Brooke Castillo's teaching on this.

Do B-minus work.

Don't strive for the A. Don't strive for perfection. Satisfy yourself with less than perfection, and get your work into the world. B-minus work is better than no work and no influence. I really want this book to be A+++ level work, but the only way I can let it go into the world is to allow it to be "good enough." If I wait until it's perfect, you'll never get to read it.

When I think about running BizChix Live again, I often become overwhelmed with the possibility that I could fail.

Maybe I won't make it as meaningful the second time.

Maybe the seats won't fill.

Maybe no one will show up.

(Nevermind that over 75% of seats were already filled within a week of the first BizChix Live ending. When you're in that place, logic doesn't always enter the equation, which is why the R.E.S.E.T. Framework is so successful.)

When that fear of failure—or the need for perfectionism— comes knocking, I go back to my breath. After breathing through it, I remember to find comfort in knowing I've done a live event before. Then I look at my past success as a win. I self-comfort if I have to and say, "It's going to be okay, Nat. We can do this."

Another way to help work through these crippling fears is to bring in data. What are the numbers now? What were they last time? What is my actual margin of error?

Sometimes, I go to worst-case scenario and ask myself, *what is the thing I fear the most?* When I identify what looms beneath all the fear, I can often say, *that's not so bad.* Or at least realize that no matter how deep the fear, I could live through it coming about.

You can live your life and run your business on fear, but not for very long, and not very deeply. If you fail?

Congratulations.

So have all of us.

Chapter 7
Fear of Success

> "I'm doing everything I can to sabotage my career.
> It's a little thing called 'Fear of Success.'"
> —*Jon Stewart, comedian, television host, and producer*

Most women—and entrepreneurs—can tell you that they have a fear of failure. Who doesn't? No one wants to pour their heart into something just to have it fail. What many either can't, or won't tell you is that they also have a fear of success.

It's not quite deep enough to say that we're afraid of success.

When I first heard about fear of success, I was shocked. It had never occurred to me. I am very achievement-oriented and always looking to do the next big thing and be ahead of my peers. The idea of someone holding themselves back for any reason was foreign to me.

After talking many women through their fears of success, I realized it's deeper than it sounds.

Fear of success is a varied, complicated issue that splinters out much like a spiderweb. At the core, it's basically the same, but it funnels into different areas. When we fear success, we actually fear our own sense of belonging and safety.

What is Fear of Success?

Fear of success dives into our most vulnerable places. It is more about how our success may impact our current relationships and might threaten our primal need to be loved and accepted.

For example—some women are afraid to be more successful than their partner because it may ultimately end their relationship. Every time this comes up, I direct them back to their partner to ask their actual (not assumed) viewpoint and to report back. The partner almost always says, "Do it! Make more money!"

Don't be afraid to ask.

I have a friend who would pay herself the exact same amount as her husband's salary. Literally to the penny. I remember asking why her revenue in her business was so high yet her take home was proportionally low. It turns out she was unconsciously spending any additional amount within her business on expensive coaching programs, additional software, updating her website, etc., so that she would not exceed her husband's take home pay.

She was worried that if she made more, it would negatively impact their relationship. After we peeled back all the layers, she was ultimately worried he would leave her if she was more successful.

Well, she was wrong!

Her husband said he would love it if she could make more. Over the next few years, her increased income helped pay off all of their debt and now they are building up a large savings, traveling more, making home improvements and have money for their kid's college.

Fear of success is often about fearing the *consequences* of success as well. Women hold themselves back because they're afraid of what success could change in their life. The consequences could be positive or negative. Maybe both! The change could be positive because the business grows, but some of their close relationships lose connection. Fear of success almost always comes back to our core relationships with other people.

Another fact of the matter here: as you change and grow, some of your friendships and relationships may change and grow too. Some people are in our lives for a lifetime and some are in our lives for a season. Seasonal friendships may shift, and acknowledging and grappling with that can be tricky.

Sometimes we have goals and plans and dreams for our business, yet just as we are close to attaining them, they disappear. We fail. Things fall apart. All of a sudden, we're too busy. Fear of success leads to procrastination or even depression. But it's more than procrastination.

Fear of success can cause you to sabotage yourself so that you're not successful.

How Do I Know?

Here are a few questions that may help you identify whether you have a fear of success.

1. Do you hold yourself back because you're stressed about creating new products to equal or surpass your current ones?
2. Are you afraid of what people in your life will say to you once you achieve your goals?
3. Does the idea of change make you sick to your stomach?
4. Are you afraid of impacting too many people?
5. Are you afraid your reach could spiral into a depth you don't control?
6. Do you get in your own way?
7. Are you afraid of making more money than your partner? Your family? Your friends?

Did any of those sound familiar?

You Are In Control

In Japan, there's a high-speed bullet train called the Shinkansen that I rode when I visited Japan after college. It has a max speed of 150-200 mph (240-320 km/hr). When you're riding that train, the world seems as if it is literally flying past you. There have been times when I've thought, "I feel like my business is on the Shinkansen." We are flying *fast*.

Fear of success is a lot like the Shinkansen. There are moments when you think you can't keep up with the momentum you feel. It starts to feel like you can't manage the impact and expectations that come with growth, income, production, hiring staff, etc.

But here's the truth about your business: **you control that train.**

No one else is conducting the bullet train. You are the driver of *your* business. You can say no to anything you want. You can pick and choose who you do work for or who works for you. At the end of the day, you are in complete control of everything that's happening in your business.

Knowing that sometimes makes it a little easier to breathe.

Sometimes the decisions we make feel like forever decisions. They aren't. Remember: we're CEO's of our own business! We are in control. We can reverse, slow down, stop that train. Or we can get off.

Motivational speaker and author Denis Waitley put it best when he said, "Procrastination is the fear of success. People procrastinate because they are afraid of the success that they know will result if they move ahead now. Because success is heavy, carries a responsibility with it, it is much easier to procrastinate and live on the 'someday I'll' philosophy."

On the flip side, we're also in control of sabotaging our success unintentionally.

Are you procrastinating getting your train going? Have there been products or tasks that you aren't getting to, or continue to fail to do, and you can't think of why?

This might be a good time to sit down and ask if there's something you're afraid of on the other side.

Meet Karen DeYoung

Karen DeYoung has been running a six-figure business for a long time—she first started her business over twenty years ago. She runs a consulting company[†] that helps manage talent and organization development for nonprofit government agencies. She started out part-time while her kids were little so she could enjoy the flexibility of working for herself. Over time, she grew into an established business with employees that is well on the way to the seven-figure mark.

Karen is a wildly successful female entrepreneur, who—guess what?—also struggles with fear of success.

"Will people still love me?" she asks herself when she thinks about the ramifications of being successful. "Will I still fit in? Will I be separate? All those things go through my mind. Will I be alone?"

For Karen, her fear of success is most apparent in her relationships with other people, which is a common thread. With fear of success comes the fear of how we'll be perceived by the people that we love and care about. Remember how our childhood and memories affect our adult mindset? Families that don't accept people with a certain level of income tend to spur this kind of a mindset issue in women I work with.

Not only does Karen fear how she'll be perceived by friends and

---

[†] Visit www.youngconsultingservices.com to learn more about Karen or see a video of her interview at www.bizchix.com/RESET

loved ones, but she fears how hitting the high marks she sets for herself will change her life and relationships.

"That [fear of success] is still a journey—that's not something I've completed. A lot of [management of] it for me is around the people that I'm with."

Karen has found more safety in talking to her business peers about her business success. Her non-business friends are at a different place in life. Many of them are nearing retirement or have careers they aren't passionate about—and that's okay. But it's her husband that has posed the trickiest viewpoint to manage.

In fact, he didn't want her to make more money when she first set the goal to increase from $100,000 a year to $200,000.

Her husband runs a nonprofit focused on social justice. For him, it's not desirable to have a lot of money because it's a sort of antithesis to what he believes. "We don't need any more money," he said when she told him about her goal to double her income.

She had to explain that it's about a goal, not necessarily about the money. She's trying to achieve more, continually grow, and reach a new level in everything she does.

Sometimes, when working with others' fear of success in our life, we simply have to figure out a way to present our goals in a palatable way that they can appreciate. It almost always comes down to communication—both with yourself and those you care about.

Coping with Success

Sometimes, we have to learn how to experience success.

"I partially felt like there wasn't room for me," attorney Danielle Liss said when I last spoke with her about fear of success. "I wasn't going to be successful if I couldn't achieve this random thing I had fixated on. It was a battle in my head. It was a battle between trying to feel it and being down in it."

Danielle had to learn, like so many of us do, that there is room for us at the table. When we get there? Enjoy it. Lean back. Savor the moment. Make a plan. Talk to your supportive friends, or find a biz bestie that understand your desires to grow your business. Trust yourself to continue to achieve.

Danielle and Karen aren't the only ones that have struggled with coping with their success. My client Taryn Holstrom, who runs Skagit

Valley Wedding Rentals[†] spoke with me on my podcast about fearing what success would require her to do.

"I fear a little bit of success," she admitted in an on-air coaching call.[‡] "Not in the sense of the money that comes with it, but the time that I'm going to have to dedicate to get that success."

Taryn has two children under the age of five and is comfortable working ten to fifteen hours per week. She doesn't want to work forty to seventy hours a week (which she's done in the past before she had children). Her fear is that growing too big, and having too much success, would require more work.

In other words: change.

"There's something in my mind that's keeping me from seeing how [growth] is possible," she said.

Managing time, family, and business flow can get really tricky—especially when scaling your business is part of the landscape. Your business can grow; you can hire people, maintain profit, and not have to work more than you want to. Because it's your business, you control that growth. If it's becoming overwhelming, you can back up. The change success may (or may not) bring is scalable.

A more successful business doesn't have to change your life or relationships. That train is yours to drive, just like Taryn found out.

What I've noticed is that some women don't know what they would do with the success. When that comes up, I always ask, "What would it change if you had more success in a positive way?"

Bring this response to the forefront as a motivational force. Then consciously decide to do whatever you're doing.

I don't want you avoiding a fear, but making a concrete, intentional decision. A lot of this book will bring to the surface things that spin in the back of our mind. The very things that impact our behaviors and decisions.

For example—Karen's family isn't really needing more money. They aren't chasing a larger lifestyle, but there are things that success can do for them and each of us:

- Enable greater impact and ability to serve more people
- Impact our community by creating jobs

[†] Visit www.skagitvalleyweddingrentals.com to see Taryn's business in action.

[‡] If you want to hear the podcast, check out https://bizchix.com/291-on-air-coaching-fear-of-success-with-taryn-holmstrom/

- Allow us to support other family members
- Contribute to nonprofits and charities
- Create a scholarship
- Provide clean water
- Build a school

Couple Success with Failure

There's a reason this chapter comes after the chapter on fear of failure. When you're facing your fears on failure, it can be helpful to think about your possible fears of success at the same time.

Instead of asking how you'd feel if the project went bad, figure out how you'd feel if it went *well*. What if you succeeded beyond your wildest imagination? What would that mean? Where would it put your business? How would it change the landscape? Not only may this help you anticipate possible routes of procrastination, but it could help you overcome your fear of failure to see what could go well.

Of course, don't overwhelm yourself with dealing with fear of failure and fear of success if it feels like too much. Sometimes, however, the two can balance each other out.

Chapter 8
Fear of Judgment

"Doubt yourself and you doubt everything you see. Judge yourself and you see judges everywhere. But if you listen to the sound of your own voice, you can rise above doubt and judgment. And you can see forever."

—*Nancy Lopez, retired American professional golfer*

The fear of judgment is a crippling place to be. Judgment is tied into our self-esteem, decision-making, worldview, inner thought life, you name it. We're born without fear of judgment—no baby apologizes for the way they look or things they say. Even toddlers who dance wild or act crazy and with abandon have no fear of how others will judge them. Somewhere along the way, we learn to fear the opinions of others.

Or our own judgment.

Fear of judgment is a learned thing. In fact, there's a name for it: allodoxaphobia. The fear of hearing other people's opinions. What you'll find about fear of judgment is quite interesting. It's rolled up into many of the other issues we can face, like fear of failure or fear of success. Sometimes it's an onerous trio and you can have all three at the same time around the same issue.

In fact, you could have *all* the mindset issues we talk about in this book.

As young kids, we believe that we're artists. We color, create, sculpt, draw, and believe in ourselves. Then the world tells us that we're not ... but maybe we still are.

When we're in kindergarten, we're just drawing and making our own art in our own way. What does it matter what anyone thinks?

At some point, we decide it does.

As a coach, I've seen the fear of judgment play out in many ways, and I want to unpack it here. However it shows up in our lives, it can be crippling and difficult to work through. The secret is in knowing that you can unlearn judgment—and the fear of it.

Judging Others

First, we need to look inward.

Are you judging others?

Are you placing judgment on yourself?

We need to look inside and see if we're judging other people.

The Positivity Solution website has a beautiful article that highlights an equally beautiful truth: **we usually judge others in the areas we feel weakest.**[19]

Are you struggling to lose weight and find yourself being particularly harsh with the way other people eat or exercise?

Are you nitpicking a friend's Instagram feed—but secretly feel jealous over how many followers they have?

When I found out my ex-husband had been cheating on me, it crippled me. Every time I went into public, I felt like everyone was judging me. Some of them definitely were. When I did some inner work at that time, I realized that I was actually judging other people a lot too. I realized I have no idea what's going on in other people's homes and lives—just as they didn't know what was happening in mine.

Over time, I've gotten to a place where I can be more open-minded and less judgmental of myself and others. I try to detach myself from it. Who am I to judge? That's not my job. I stay focused on my lane and my world.

It opens up a lot of mental space.

If you're prone to gossip, you're probably being judgmental.

> **"If you're not part of the problem or solution, you shouldn't be talking about it."**
> —*Rick Warren, pastor and speaker.*

When we move away from judging others, we'll often move away from judging ourselves so harshly. It may be time to decide whose judgments really matter to you because we can't entirely remove the fact that we care about what people think of us.

Create a practice of giving grace to more people. You'll find it easier to be less concerned about others judging you.

Self-Judgment

When it comes to judging ourselves, this is where our Inner Mean Girl finds the spotlight.

Self-judgment is a lot like beating ourselves up for being human. We put labels on ourselves by saying, *I'll always be stupid*, or *I'll never be as smart as her*. Self-judgment can masquerade as limiting beliefs, or it can be a by-product of fear of success or fear of failure.

Because it's so powerful and applicable here, I'm going to repeat Timothy Gallway's quote from his book *The Inner Game of Tennis*.

"The first inner skill to be developed in the Inner Game is that of nonjudgmental awareness. When we 'unlearn' judgment we discover, usually with some surprise, that we don't need the motivation of a reformer to change our 'bad' habits. We may simply need to be more aware. There is a more natural process of learning and performing waiting to be discovered. It is waiting to show what it can do when allowed to operate without interference from the conscious strivings of the judgmental self."

Judgment from Your Friends and Family

Do you remember attorney Danielle Liss from Chapter Five?

After she listened to the podcast that destroyed her planned trajectory for her online legal business, she wallowed for a bit. In that time, she knew she needed to reach out to someone for help. This is what she told me about finding someone else (who ended up being me!).

"I wanted to talk to a stranger. I didn't want to talk to anyone else ... I was afraid that my partner would judge me, my husband would judge me. My biggest fear was that someone would say, *You left a company at a C level position, and you're dumb. Why would you do that?*"

Sometimes, our fear of judgment from other people can be a block to successfully working through mindset issues. If you feel this is the case for you—you don't want to talk to the people in your life because of fear of judgment—I want to encourage you to find someone else. A coach. A therapist. A mentor. Someone not emotionally attached to the outcome so that you can trust them to withhold judgment and not give advice based upon emotion.

You can set this situation up for success. All you have to do is say, "I'm having a mindset issue that I need to talk about, and I'm afraid of people judging me for it. Can I talk to you about it without worrying about that?"

If that seems too scary to do to someone in your life, especially in person, reach out over email or any other means that does feel safe until you can work through those emotions.

Let's also revisit consultant Karen DeYoung for a minute, whom you met in the last chapter.

Because of her success, Karen had already struggled in managing some of the relationships in her life. She feared how more success would change how she would be perceived by the people she loved, and if it would change their relationship.

"It can be scary just to ask," she said.

She's right! It can be.

Fortunately, Karen is really good at seeking out other people who do understand. There's no reason we have to leave our current friend group to be understood—but sometimes we need to alter our expectations a little bit, the way she did. Some friends are connected to one section of our life, and we only talk to them about that section. For example, a business friend may only speak to us about business. Or we may have a mom friend who we talk mostly about our kids with. On occasion, we have a life friend that we can talk to about anything.

It's okay to have these segments. Don't expect everyone to speak into or appreciate your business. Don't give everyone the opportunity to judge.

When you're dealing with fear of judgment over a mindset issue or a decision for your business, seek out those who are supportive. Ones that have their own business and will understand the need to withhold judgment when you need it most.

Guess what? Even Oprah has some fear of judgment. "I never thought of myself as ambitious before," she said in an interview she conducted with Reese Witherspoon and Mindy Kaling on one of her SuperSoul Podcast episodes.[20] "But I feel like I needed to defend being ambitious because it was spoken to me as if it were a dirty word."

People will judge us. Friends will judge us. That's more about them and their issues.

You keep going.

> **What other people think about me is not my business.**
> —*Natalie Eckdahl*

Judgment from Your Community

Some women socialize in communities that don't support the idea of women making more money than their husbands and/or working outside the home. These women often tell me it feels too "indulgent" to make as much as, or more than, their husband. Or to have their kids in daycare while they are at work.

Other women have communities where all their friends are stay-at-home-moms and those mom's judge working moms. We're not here to demean any woman because of her choice. Being a stay-at-home-mom is hard work! (I've done it.) But for the woman who wants to work *and* be a mom, having friends that don't share that belief system can be very isolating.

There can be a lot of pressure in some circles for women to stay out of the career field and exclusively in the home. I've even met women who run their businesses from home and still introduce themselves as stay-at-home moms even though they run significant businesses. They don't feel they have permission to share that they own a business without being judged for it.

It's especially tricky for women in these communities when the family doesn't need the income and their ideal lifestyle is currently being supported by their partner. These women are often really quiet about their success. Other women say to them, "Why would you work when you don't have to?"

One of my clients has a six-figure business and is starting another future six-figure business, yet she never shares with her mom friends about her level of success. She hears them talk about other women in a judgmental way, so she doesn't give them the opportunity to do the same to her.

Judgment from Your Industry

Yoga teacher and consultant Shannon Crow (you first met her in Chapter Five) spoke with me about the difficulty of judgment from an entire *industry*.

Turns out ... it can be pretty intense. There's a lot of judgment in her community around hustling, marketing, or "pushing" people into yoga.

"In the yoga world," Shannon said, "there's a feeling that you should give things away for free or deliver your services and charge the lowest price possible."

This applies to anyone in a helping profession—it's not just a yoga industry thing. Other clients have spoken with me about this as well: speech therapists, psychologists, marriage and family therapists, nurses, etc.

Not only do some female entrepreneurs feel as if they shouldn't be charging well for what they do, but people in their industry are judging them for getting paid as well!

The fear of judgment here is: *I can't do this because my industry thinks it's wrong or bad, which means I'm a bad person.*

Fear of judgment can be so powerful it haunts each decision, especially in helping industries. "That [fear of judgment] even happens when I talk about building my email list or putting out a Facebook ad," Shannon told me.

To this, I want to point out several things that Shannon used to help her work through the fear of judgment in the yoga industry.

1. **Remember your value.** There are people who will pay to work with you. Even in the yoga world! For Shannon, she had to realize that there were people that would pay $100 for a one-on-one class with her, for example.

2. **You can't impact more people if you go out of business.** If you aren't charging enough, you can't keep your doors open. There are many yoga teachers that struggle because they're afraid to be seen as someone who is hustling or advertising. Shannon said it best when she told me, "There's really no *pushing* someone into doing yoga."

3. **It's okay if everyone doesn't want to work with you.** If you're running a consultancy business, keep in mind what Shannon learned: you don't want to work with people that don't want to move their business forward. For Shannon, she learned to be okay if they weren't attracted to her message. Her message? *Do you want to create a sustainable and profitable business? Because that is what will continue to help people.*

If there is someone—or many people—in your industry that are still judging you, then I say this: ignore them. Judgments from others says far more about them than it does about you. I learned long ago that I needed to take a step back and realize that judgment on any level is more about the person doing the judging.

PMS

Our self-judgment and mindset issues in general can be amplified during certain points in our menstrual cycles. I often counsel the women I work with, when they're going through a self-imposed shame storm, to check in with their monthly cycles.

One of my clients that you'll meet more in-depth later, Tara Humphrey, has noticed she's most vulnerable around her period. She spoke with her doctor about it, who was able to suggest some herbal supplements that have noticeably helped her. I've observed it in my own life too.

While there's not a lot you can do to totally control the swing of emotions that comes with being female, the awareness often brings a little reprieve. Or at least informs that it's time to step back and do a little more self-care.

We all know that when it's that time; the Inner Mean Girl has a much louder voice.

Six Quick Tips

When it comes to fear of judgment, as with all mindset issues, there is hope! Here are six quick tips that will get you well on your way to dealing with this mindset issue.

1. **Start with you.** Are you judging others? Be mindful of your judgmental behavior and work to reduce it.
2. **Choose your five VIP's carefully.** Who are the five people whose input and thoughts are to be valued highest right now?
3. **Look for an objective mentor.** Choose someone that you can talk these things out with, and who isn't emotionally connected to the situation.
4. **Give yourself a long-term perspective.** Will those opinions you're afraid of matter in one week? One year? Ten years?
5. **Work on your strong mental game.** When you identify fear of judgment, dig into the root of it. Go to the worst-case scenario. Figure out what would happen if someone you love or whose approval you value didn't validate your decision.

6. **Check in with your hormones.** Do you need a little more self-care right now? Do you need to table these thoughts for a few days? Whatever you need, don't be afraid to do it. Take care of yourself. Judgment free.

Chapter 9
Limiting Beliefs

> "I'm not interested in your limiting beliefs; I'm interested in what makes you limitless."
> —*Brendon Buchard, High Performance Coach and best-selling author*

A limiting belief is when you impose limits on yourself and the things you can and cannot do. It's a protective mechanism; we don't want to suffer pain. If we shoot low when we know we can do it, we won't be disappointed.

Remember talking about our lizard brain when we discussed the concept of "shipping" with Seth Godin? Our amygdala wants to protect us from harm and keep us from getting hurt. Our brain is actually encouraging us to limit ourselves

In allowing that, we won't really live, either.

Limiting beliefs often sound like this:

> *I could never do that.*
> *No client would ever pay me that.*
> *That's not possible.*
> *I was lucky, and luck never lasts.*
> *I don't have time.*
> *I'll never figure this out.*
> *Other people can do it better than I can.*
> *I'm too old.*
> *I'm too young.*
> *I could never reach that level.*
> *Things never work out for me.*
> (see more at the end of this chapter from women in the BizChix community)

My client Jacqueline Snyder (you'll hear more from her later) said it best when she told me, "I think they're things that you tell yourself all the time that you don't realize you're telling yourself all the time."

It's scientifically proven[21] that the amount we believe in ourselves is directly proportional to our success rate. In fact, studies[22] have shown that our self-beliefs influence our choice of career, to a negative or positive effect.

> "Whether you think you can, or whether you think you can't, you will."
> —Henry Ford, founder of the Ford Motor Company.

VIP Days

When I launched the BizChix podcast in 2014, I made $0 that year. I was running another business and gave birth to my 3rd child as well.

In 2015, I began coaching and hosting masterminds and started making a modest income. The women in the mastermind I attended (not the one I hosted) started encouraging me to offer a VIP day in my business. They said women in my audience would pay thousands of dollars to fly out to California and spend the day with me so I could immerse myself in their business and help them achieve a big goal or conquer a problem they faced.

When they proposed I start this, I could not conceptualize that people would want to spend an entire day with me.

A year and a half passed.

Finally, I decided to offer it. In January of 2017, my first VIP client flew out from Canada to work with me. It was a big journey for her! We dug deep into her business and uncovered things that would have been difficult to uncover any other way. I can look back now and know that people would have done a VIP day in that year and a half time when I was sitting on the idea. People were waiting!

But I trapped myself in a limiting belief.

The part of imposing these limitations for myself that stings the most is missing the ability to help other women overcome their challenges and move forward in their business through VIP days.

When we limit ourselves, we may be limiting others too.

The Law of Averages

Nonprofit consultant Karen De Young also struggled with limiting beliefs, but in a different way. She found that many of her long-term friendships were talking about limiting beliefs in their lives, and *she* was picking up on them for herself.

For her, the question she grappled with was, *How can I be with my long-term relationships, hear their limiting beliefs, and not let them come into my head?*

These people are very important to her. She values the shared history together and the other ways they positively impact her life.

In fact, let's revisit Jim Rohn[23] from when he spoke of the *law of averages*. He said, "You are the average of the five people you spend the most time with."

I like to reframe this to be you are the average of the five people whose opinions/teachings/mentorship you give the most weight to.

Who you allow to speak into your life matters.

This is something I believe Karen understood fundamentally, but maybe not consciously. She knew that the long-term relationships in her life had limiting beliefs they lived by, and she didn't want to be influenced by them.

How do you manage that?

For Karen, it came back (yet again!) to having an outlet where she could be her authentic self with that part of her life.

Surrounding herself with like-minded entrepreneurs kept the reminders fresh that she can do whatever she dreams, she doesn't have to limit herself, and her potential has no bounds. Not only that, but she has a conscious awareness of limiting beliefs, and that she doesn't have to adopt them.

When she hears limiting beliefs from other people now, it doesn't affect her. She doesn't internalize their beliefs. It doesn't change her behavior. It makes her less inclined to share her visions or dreams with certain people, but that's okay. It's not what that group of people is for. She has a group of likeminded female entrepreneurs where she can discuss her business goals and dreams.

The Power of Competition

Sometimes, all it takes is a little competition to erase a limiting belief.

R.E.S.E.T. Your Mindset

I've observed people working through their mindset issues since I was a teenager. My first business was teaching private swimming lessons in high school and college. A lot of people had pools in their backyards in our neighborhood and beyond, and I was a competitive swimmer and a natural with kids. My mom encouraged me to start the business and even helped me get my first clients. In truth, she was my first business coach and salesperson. (Thanks Mom!)

I could teach almost any child to swim within two weeks—some within one—but I had some kids that were really scared. They didn't want to swim or they didn't believe they could swim. Guess what? Even learning to swim is about mindset.

It's about believing that you can swim and having confidence to try. After I taught someone the basics, and they could hold themselves up, it was all about whether they thought they could swim.

Four-year-old Ethan and his best friend Evan were two of my clients.

Evan learned quickly and was fearless. He wasn't afraid of the deep end or going under water. Ethan, however, struggled. He would only go in the deep end if I held his hand. Was he capable of swimming in the deep end without my help? Absolutely. However, he didn't think he could.

I had exhausted all the tools in my belt to help someone overcome a mindset issue (although I didn't call it that then) and so I invited Evan to join our lesson. We decided to go into the deep end with Evan. We started swimming. Evan was on my right, swimming on his own. Ethan was on my left and holding my hand. Halfway through, Ethan looked over and saw his BFF swimming by himself.

Guess what?

Ethan let go of my hand.

He literally pushed it away.

From that moment on, Ethan swam in the deep end all by himself.

It reminds me of the quote, *"She believed she could, so she did,"* by R.S. Grey. Ethan believed he could do it, so he did. The only thing holding him back was himself. You know what? That happens to all of us. Sometimes, you're the only one holding you back. Like Ethan, I've observed that just knowing something is possible, or seeing someone else do it, is enough to spur us to action.

Others' Limiting Beliefs

Many of you don't have people supporting your entrepreneurial journey. These individuals operate with a limiting belief system ... and they're putting it on you.

That alone can create limiting beliefs in you that are very hard to face down. Please know that you are not alone.

Many of my clients struggle with getting full support from their family and friends. The levels vary. Your partner may not think it's a great idea that you start this new business, but is okay with you trying ... for a while. Your parents may think you're crazy and constantly opine that you should do something "stable." I hear you.

This journey isn't easy, but it isn't impossible.

Don't spend precious time convincing them to change *their* limiting beliefs. Instead of wasting energy on people who have already made up their minds, bring other people into your life that support you. It's okay if your naysayers just don't get it.

Don't let them hold you back.

Prove to them what you can do by doing it. Your partner or family will become much more supportive if they start to reap the benefits.

Another thing that can help is for you to stop for a few minutes and take a pulse on your life. Are you difficult to live with because of the business?

Absent?

Is a partner or a child or parent taking on too much so you can have the dream? Is zero or limited money coming back to your personal bank account?

Communication and realignment can go a long way in bridging some of those gaps. Not to mention help you identify potential sources of limiting beliefs and work through your long-term relationships so the limiting beliefs aren't impacting you (or them!) so deeply.

They Won't Pay That Much

One area where I see limiting beliefs is in terms of what we charge. Almost all women need to charge more! We become entrepreneurs to escape things like outside control and working for other people, but we create a glass ceiling for ourselves with limiting beliefs around what others will pay. (More on this in the next chapter.)

We're literally doing it to ourselves.

We definitely—and often subconsciously—create a range in our head about what people will pay us for what we offer.

Some of these may sound familiar:

> *No one would pay that.*
> *I can't charge that much.*
> *Who has that kind of money?*
> *I'm not worth that price.*
> *I wouldn't pay for that.*
> *Who am I to charge that?*

It's a limiting belief that people won't pay a certain amount for your service or product. The people that really value the transformation you are offering will find the money to pay. Your job is to make the offer and let other people make the decision regarding whether they want to work with you. It's not your job to decide whether they will or will not take it.

Think of it in terms of my example: because I waited over a year and a half to offer the VIP day, I limited my influence and force for good in the world. I limited growth in my business, myself, and possible impact on my family.

Do you want that?

Also consider this: once you're making what you want to be making, you can decide how you contribute to better the world. You can offer scholarships to people in need. There are so many ways to give back. If you're playing into those limiting beliefs about what you charge, then the day will come when you can't keep doing what you're meant to be doing.

You'll also find that limiting beliefs come into play around thought leadership in a similar way. I often see women create a limiting belief that they are not the person to claim thought leadership. To put their systems out there. That is for someone else. *I couldn't be known. I couldn't be as great as so-and-so.*

You can.

And you should.

The Inner Mean Girls Scripts

Limiting beliefs are scripts playing in your head.

The phrases, sentences, and words roll through like a ticker tape—and you may not even realize it. Some of them come from our past. Some may have originated from recent fears or failures. They build up a lot of our inner thought life and involve what you believe about yourself . . . and your potential for success.

What we say to ourselves is very powerful.

And often really mean.

Have you said things to yourself that you would never say to anyone else? Are you replaying things that a parent or caregiver said about you? You may have seen a relationship where success in business or a career impacted the relationship—and not in a good way. Did you have pragmatic parents that didn't believe in taking risks or stepping out of their comfort zone?

To help illustrate this, I asked the female entrepreneurs in my Facebook group to tell me some of the mean thoughts in their heads. I'm going to be honest—these were sobering and difficult to read. But I think it's important that you see how normal some of these thoughts are if you're experiencing them yourself.

Actual Limiting Beliefs

- Anything you think of saying has already been said—and much better than you can say it.
- If people really knew you, they would not like you.
- Those people saying nice things about you are so sweet, but they just don't know you well enough to see how crummy you are.
- What are you even trying to do?
- She has more experience than you do.
- She writes better than you do.
- How come you can't be more like her?
- You have to do it the "right way".
- No wonder she's more successful . . . look at all she's done.
- Who would want to listen to you since you can't talk or speak like her?
- You are never going to be able to do everything you are aiming for.
- You set so many goals, but then, really, you never go for them.
- You just keep all these things in your head, but they will never be more than that, and you are hurting your own life.

- You just want too much.
- How can I teach others to improve themselves when I am not perfect at what I teach?
- You're not pretty enough/thin enough/young enough to be on camera.
- This project is going to fail.
- It's not good enough.
- You will never be a part of THE elite group in your niche.
- Everyone is laughing at you.
- You will never break through and attain that big goal.
- It's too late for you to try to make it big.
- You waited too long.
- You're not qualified or suited for your position.
- No one wants your product.
- You can't do this.
- Why even try if it won't ever work?
- You're not worthy of being paid money.
- You don't fit into your industry.
- You're too much of an advocate to be taken seriously as a scientist, or the fact that you're not a man.
- Your product . . . really? C'mon . . . no one wants to buy it.
- You're living on your retirement; you're 40, and you need to get your life together.
- Who do you think you are?
- You can't just fire a client!
- You can't afford to lose clients.
- You're not ever going to do well no matter how much you make because you will mess it up somehow.
- You are not a good boss because you drop the ball.
- Your success is not sustainable.
- You don't know anything, really.
- You suck at business.
- You are kidding yourself that people will pay you for your services.

I never end on a low note, so I asked all of those women to tell me how they silenced their Inner Mean Girl. Here are a few things that they do to quiet that voice. Tuck these into your back pocket for those really bad days.

Silencing Strategies

- I try to cancel the negative talk and replace it immediately with a positive affirmation, sometimes while looking at myself in the mirror.
- I practice meditation 10+ minutes a day.
- I am very possessive of my evening "decompression time".
- Vegging with Netflix while having a cup of decaf.
- I pray.
- I have faith that I am blessed and that things always work out in my favor.
- I listen to motivational podcasts and try not to put attention on negative things.
- I surround myself with people I want to emulate, whom I respect and respect me.
- I try so hard to reframe things in my mind so I'm looking at things differently. For example, if I'm at a conference and I think a person is ignoring me and not wanting to converse, I try to think of reasons of why she might be doing that. Like *she's probably thinking about her presentation, or maybe she's feeling overwhelmed.*
- Reading.
- Attending events.
- Working on applying the knowledge and guidance I garner.
- Have an open notepad and immediately write those thoughts down.
- I repeat "I am courage" over and over again.

You can silence those limiting beliefs. Here are a few more helpful hints to help you along the way.

1. **Pick a new script.** Let's say your old script is this, *There's no way I can create a product as good as or better than my last one.* There's an underlying fear of expectations and fulfillment here. Instead of convincing yourself you can't do it, another script would be, *I am a creative professional. Good ideas are abundant. I am always improving.*
2. **Maintain your new script.** This is a great time to change your environment. Put your new script on a post it note, and tack

it onto your bathroom mirror, your steering wheel, and the compact in your purse. Change your computer desktop. Your phone background. Tell your partner or your kids. Saying it out loud can be very affirming. Meditate on your new script. Write it down over and over again.
3. **Recognize a relapse.** There are some days when I can feel that (or those!) limiting belief coming back. That means I need to do some work with my new script to make it more powerful than ever.

Warning: we're all going to relapse from time to time with our limiting beliefs.

When it happens, create a more powerful belief system. Don't avoid it; dig in. Try journaling. Talk it out with someone. *Why* do you have that limiting belief? Why is it haunting you now?

Our inner thought life is connected to everything in our business in intricate ways. Once we dig up the roots and tendrils, we can pull that weed and plunk a new flower in its place.

I have the privilege of seeing into a lot of women's minds and experiences. I know what you're going through, and your courage is astounding. All of you are experiencing it on some level. You can do this.

You are worthy of success. You are powerful. You are amazing at what you do. Money and success are abundant for you and your business.

You've got this.

Chapter 10
Money Mindset

> "What we really want to do is what we are really meant to do. When we do what we are meant to do, money comes to us, doors open for us, we feel useful, and the work we do feels like play to us."
> —*Julia Cameron, author of "The Artist's Way"*

One of the most talked about issues among the women entrepreneurs in my community revolves around money mindset.

It's hard (READ: impossible) to run a business well without working on your money mindset, especially in the beginning. If you struggle with money on a variety of levels—whether that's mindset, managing it, or investing it—this chapter is for you.

One of the most important things for you to know is this: you are not alone in your money mindset issues. In fact, this topic is so encompassing it could be an entire book on its own. (Hmm . . . food for thought.) I would be remiss to ignore it here, so we're going to dive into the basics.

Many people struggle with their relationship regarding money, wealth, or prosperity. I'm going to spotlight several female entrepreneurs and their money struggles (some of them you've met in previous chapters). I feel like it's important to normalize this experience, and stories resonate. The most common money mindset issues that I see will be covered here, and then I'll tell you a story about a woman that has worked with (or still is working through) that issue.

Let's start with me.

My Money Mindset Story

I grew up in a home where my parents were conservative about money, but money didn't feel scarce. My mom was an adaptive PE teacher and my dad was a civil engineer for the government. Early in elementary school, my dad started his own business with two partners. We had enough to do the things we wanted to do, and we lived in a town that was a primarily blue collar, working class town. I didn't know people that had a lot more or a lot less. As my dad's business grew, we moved more toward upper middle class. In high school, my family moved to a new city and built a custom home.

My mom saw value in investing in our activities, so we did a lot of things like private swimming and piano lessons. We bought new clothes from modest stores, and we always had a budget. When I was younger, our family vacations were camping, but as our family income increased, we started renting places at the beach and were able to travel to Disney World in Florida to visit family.

Scarcity didn't enter my life until high school.

My grandfather was an entrepreneur in a second-generation family cement business, and a jovial guy that truly loved to have fun. My memories involve water skiing behind his boat and camping with him in his motorhome, which felt like a big upgrade from our family tent camping! He was a bright person and life of the party, who didn't focus much on the future. In fact, my grandma said that his focus was getting his work crews started in the morning so they could theoretically run on their own and he could go golfing.

He died suddenly of a heart attack when I was a senior in high school, leaving my grandma with a lot of debt and uncertainty.

When he died, he had no savings, tons of payments, and a tiny life insurance policy. My grandmother had to sell the beloved motorhome, get roommates in her three-bedroom house, and later take on a babysitting job, just to make ends meet. That was my first introduction to the unexpected way life can shift from normalcy to scarcity.

Fast forward to college.

My parents had planned to help me pay for my college education, and it certainly started out that way. Unfortunately, my dad's civil engineering business was highly impacted by the ups and downs of the construction industry. In the early 1990's, California hit a recession.

So did my family.

I had a partial scholarship to a private school at the time, but to help my family, I changed schools to a less expensive option and moved in with my grandma who my parents were also supporting. Then I finished school as fast as I could and graduated in two and a half years.

Normalcy to scarcity.

Fast forward to married life.

In my mind, I had my whole life figured out. My ex-husband and I were both high performing people that tended to be successful in whatever we did. I was staying at home with my baby daughter and had stopped my lucrative career as a management consultant to enjoy this special time with her. All his law school debt was paid off. We had a house and a brand new car (bought with money from my consulting business). Everything was going great. Beautiful.

Normal, if you will.

Until the rug came out again.

Right after I found out about his affair, my would-be-ex husband transferred a significant amount of money out of our joint accounts into a new account that only he had access to. Talk about nerve wracking. When our marriage finally blew up, I had a small baby and no active career. Yet again, I was left feeling that the game had been changed on me, but this time the stakes were higher. This was more than money; this was my family, my life, my emotions, and my self-esteem.

Back to scarcity.

This is my money theme that I battle. I think things are fine and then the rug gets pulled out from under me. I have to course correct. What I've learned over time is that I know how to reset. I've done a good job resetting! When things fall apart, I have to work not to fall into old patterns. Transforming our mindset is a process, even for me.

But I have learned to recognize those old scarcity feelings and focus on a positive money mindset and believing in abundance.

Money is abundant. There is more than enough for all of us.

Abandonment

Goldi's story at my first BizChix Live event literally took my breath away—it was so powerful and big.

From the stage at BizChix Live, I asked the room to share what the word *money* brings up for them and I probed about the stories they had around money. Women were raising their hands and calling out popcorn style across the room. They shared very vulnerable insights.

Then Goldi raised her hand and said, "If you make more money than your husband, he'll leave."

I had to pause to catch my breath and dig into that. When I asked her about that comment, what she revealed was even more fascinating, because her money mindset is so multifaceted.

I am grateful for Goldi expanding on this even further when I interviewed her for this book.[†]

Goldi's belief that *if you make more than your husband, he'll leave* actually stems from her own experience as a young girl when her parents divorced. Her mother, a public health nurse, had a successful career. She spoke locally at first, but her influence spread. Eventually, she was invited to speak more broadly.

Goldi's mother felt that this growth threatened Goldi's father. Not only because of the money, but also because of her growing success.

Goldi's perspective seen through the lens of a child?

This is about money.

She internalized that she should make *less* than her future husband. Which makes the next part of Goldi's story even more fascinating. When I interviewed her, she said that after BizChix Live, she realized she'd never given herself a paycheck from her own business that was more than her husband was making.

Are you noticing a theme? I've heard some version of this belief from many women in my community.

In order to disguise she was making more, Goldi would pay for family expenses out of her business without first putting the funds it into their family.

Goldi's "aha" moment at the event helped her realize that she didn't really know how her husband felt about her income. This is the perfect example of just how quickly women can move through mindset issues. From here, she was able to go through the first three steps of the R.E.S.E.T. Framework very quickly. Her first **take action** step?

She had a conversation with her husband.

As she shared her concerns, he said, "Why would you do that? I never gave you that impression. I can't wait for you to make more money!" In fact, he had been waiting for her to make the money they needed so he could pursue new dreams. Now her goal is to replace his income.

[†] To hear Goldi's full recounting in our interview, visit www.bizchix.com/RESET

She already gave herself a $3,000 raise.

Way to take action, Goldi!

This money mindset revelation also paved the way for her to have conversations with her mom about money as well.

Scarcity—Meet Jacqueline Snyder

Jacqueline Snyder's father was an entrepreneur.

Her father immigrated to the US from Morocco and started working at thirteen to financially provide for his parents and siblings. He was a serial entrepreneur and operated multiple businesses. Anytime he needed to, he could make money. Jacqueline can't recall him having a limiting belief around money—it was always accessible to him.

Her father was also a big risk taker which caused huge highs and low lows in the family finances. Sometimes they lived in opulent houses in wealthy neighborhoods, and sometimes they lived in smaller apartments in less affluent sides of town. Jacqueline recalls that they were evicted multiple times from their homes as those ebbs and flows came and went. Because of this, she attended seven elementary schools. (Keep in mind that means in six years she moved seven times.) Her greatest childhood dream was to have the same bedroom.

This lack of stability has infiltrated many of her mindset issues.

Neither Jacqueline nor her husband have the job security of a regular paycheck. He's a professional actor who works regularly on Broadway and television. She also became an entrepreneur. One riddled with money mindset issues, the greatest of them being scarcity.

As Jacqueline and I have worked together, I've often been perplexed by the depth of her scarcity fears. In fact, she gets there *really* fast!

What confuses me is that Jacqueline has a decade of experience in the fashion industry and is respected for helping clients grow their new fashion lines. She has a steady flow of referral clients and incredible SEO. New potential clients reach out to her every week.

If one of her clients isn't happy, she goes to the all-bad spot instantaneously ... even though she has other clients and stability. **The primal feeling of scarcity comes up even when there isn't scarcity.**

Remember, mindset issues are not rational and our lizard brain is constantly seeking to protect us and keep us safe.

While discussing scarcity with her, Jacqueline said, "The fear for me is that no one is ever going to work with me again. The phone is going to stop ringing ... but also that [we'll be in that] absolute worst place and run out of money, be homeless, and have to move in with my in-laws."

Let's see the R.E.S.E.T. Framework in action here.

For Jacqueline she **recognized** her issue—scarcity— and **evaluated** that it stemmed from her childhood. She created **stories about scarcity** that weren't real until she said **enough**. Now she **takes action** through finding her triggers, building a community, and working with a coach and therapist.

This mindset issue still crops up, mostly when her triggers flare, like when she has a rough day with a client. Overall, however, she's able to manage it with awareness, education, and reaching out. As Jacqueline's coach, I've tried to help her make the money more tangible. We have a shared spreadsheet that forecasts her future income and we have created longer-term contracts with all her clients. That way she can predict her income for the next six to twelve months. We've also looked at what her capacity is to take on new clients so we know how much space she has available.

The more tangible money and numbers become, the easier it is to feel more grounded.

Dealing with Scarcity

One thing that helps me through a scarcity moment is thinking about whether there's something I can take care of in that moment.

For example: is there any invoice I can pay?

Sometimes I feel like I need to hold onto all the money I have and never let it go because more money may not come. My money past tries to tell me it's safer to hoard money, even though I rationally know I have the ability to create more revenue anytime! I may feel scarcity around paying an invoice or hiring a new person, for example. When I'm feeling that tightness mentally and physically, I ask, *how can I let some money go?*

I've learned that if I send money into the world, it always comes back—and more.

The best way to deal with scarcity is to responsibly let money go.

Once I do, the money always seems to flow right back in. Often instantaneously.

Someone may book a VIP day with me. Someone will refund me money I wasn't expecting. I might make an affiliate sale. Something will happen where money comes back. Once I pay my invoices, I look at how I can bring money into my business. Is there someone I can follow up with? Am I preventing money coming in somehow? Is there someone interested in working with me?

I keep money flowing in and out of my life instead of just keeping it in. I also like to picture money moving around me, in and out, like a river. It circulates in the air and is available to take. I can reach up and grab it. I say my mantra, *money flows in and money flows out.* Try repeating it over and over with me as you take a few deep breaths in and out.

Meet Betsy Furler—Getting Help with Your Numbers

In my practice, I find that women often hesitate about getting help with their numbers.

Either they often don't enjoy it, or aren't gifted, or spend all this energy doing it (or avoiding it) instead of paying for a bookkeeper. The truth is that it doesn't cost as much as it may seem, and can save you money—or prevent mindset issues—in the end.

Let's talk about Betsy Furler.

She's an incredible entrepreneur from Houston, Texas who has run her own private speech therapist practice for twenty-six years. She recently launched her second business, *Your App Lady*,[†] which helps companies make their digital products more accessible so they reach all of their users. I've worked with her since the end of 2016 and have watched Betsy completely shift many of her mindset issues (although she's still working on some, of course!).

Because Betsy is certified and licensed to be a speech pathologist—and is used to being in a helping profession—it's been a difficult transition to owning her thought leadership as a specialist in tech where there's no certification for what she does and no clear cut ways to charge her clients.

(I often find that for women who have a certification, moving into thought leadership or mentoring can be a struggle.)

Here's her R.E.S.E.T. Framework breakdown.

---

† See more about Betsy's incredible business at https://yourapplady.com/ or see her exclusive, full interview at www.bizchix.com/RESET

She **recognized** through working with me that she had a money mindset issue about how much money she made. She **evaluated** it to be the result of transitioning from a helping profession (with a certification) to the new world of tech. She stopped telling herself the **story** that her services weren't worth charging money for. She said **enough** of that—she wanted to stay in tech—and **took action** in one area by seeking to understand the way money flows in and out of her business and her family budget.

How did she do that?

She got real with the numbers.

Betsy looked at the numbers in her business and her home by hiring a bookkeeper. For her, making decisions based on actual numbers was a game changer.

Many women with money mindset issues don't really look at—or understand—the money flowing in and out of their life. If your numbers are a mystery, money is going to feel scary. It might feel like money is scarce when it's not, or that it's abundant when it's not. Understanding the revenue, expenses, and profit in our business is key to truly moving forward with a healthy money relationship.

Our Own Ceilings

You may remember Karen, the non-profit consultant from Chapter Seven, where we discussed being afraid of success. With Karen, we can actually take that a little deeper. For her, it drives all the way to her belief systems about money.

Karen told me about a time when she was talking to a colleague in her same field. They were at a meeting of several local business owners, sharing what their business had achieved that year. Karen mentioned that she had made $100,000 that year and was looking to conservatively grow the next year. Then her colleague said that she had made $200,000 and she had also expected a bit more.

All of a sudden, she realized she'd been putting a subconscious cap on her own success. Knowing that someone else in the same field with the same level of experience had made over double meant it was possible. The fact that Karen's husband has some limiting beliefs about money that are opposite to Karen's also made this a challenging situation.

But now it was different. Karen is one of the kindest and most generous people you will ever meet, but she is a high achiever and has a competitive streak as well. Karen's not motivated by having more things, but by being her best self. She wants to achieve as much as she can possibly achieve.

Learning that her colleague was making twice what she was immediately created a new goal for her. The next year, she made it to $200,000. Her business continues to grow as her mind continues to expand. It's heading quickly to a seven-figure business.

Isn't it fascinating how quickly that can happen?

Karen said it best when she told me, "I didn't realize at the time that I had a ceiling in my mind. It's only in looking back that I realized I had a ceiling that I imposed on myself."

It's so powerful what opening the possibility of a higher goal can do for you.

Labels

Let's go back to attorney Danielle Liss for a moment.

"Money mindset was the biggest issue I didn't acknowledge I had," she said. "My money issues go deep … For me, I labeled myself as financially irresponsible in my twenties. I was, for sure, because I had a lot of stress. I was really unhappy in my previous career, and I was running up debt like crazy. I had compulsive shopping issues. I had $37,000 in credit card debt and had to do a lot of things to make it work."

So begins Danielle's money mindset story.

Danielle's label from her twenties was something she carried for a long time, which meant she filled that label constantly. Eventually, once she got a hold of her finances, she mentally maintained the belief that she was financially irresponsible, and then held on to lower, more limiting beliefs, such as *I just want enough,* and *I only need enough money to be comfortable.*

It's hard to unbury ourselves from a past that, in hindsight, really was littered and affected by money mindset issues. But Danielle is one example of how you can move past whatever belief systems you had and onto something healthier.

"I labeled myself a certain way, and it was really hard to work past that. I always assumed that I would live paycheck to paycheck."

Because of that label, she didn't trust herself with money. That affected her—and her family and business partner—for many years.

Not only did she label herself, but she also heard labels from other parts of her life.

These labels from family members and others we care about can sting and be difficult to move past.

However, taking the time to peel back the layers of your story can be life changing for your financial future.

Both/And Instead of Either/Or

One day, yoga teacher consultant Shannon Crow went shopping with her daughter to buy ten new yoga outfits for a new video project. Shopping—and investing in what she wears—had always been a struggle for her.

Shannon's daughter was really excited, but Shannon felt awkward and embarrassed by the extravagance. She thought to herself, *my yoga business is more about me helping people than buying so many new clothes.*

We already know the limiting beliefs and judgment Shannon has faced in her industry (see Chapter Eight), but she didn't realize it had extended so far into her money mindset that she didn't even want to buy new clothes for teaching yoga in her business!

She stopped and thought, *Wait. I can still help people and look good while I'm doing it.*

Guess what? Having money and helping people doesn't have to be mutually exclusive, but many people believe they have to be either/or.

In Shannon's case, she can have a really cute yoga outfit on *and* be an amazing, caring teacher. She doesn't have to be a good teacher *or* dress really cute. She can be a great teacher *and* make a fantastic income while looking stylish.

One way Shannon has battled her money mindset issues (which include more than what we've discussed in this section) was to try something truly out of the box.

She listened to a podcast about money while doing yoga.

It was purposeful; she wanted to put herself into an uncomfortable space by bringing together two things that didn't seem compatible. She's stretching her comfort level with money and yoga as a business. She's combining them as a way to take action. This is a huge growth step and a powerful avenue for therapy.

Can't Take Money

There are some women I've worked with who struggle with the transaction of accepting payment from their clients and customers. For people struggling with this, my dream for you is to work at Starbucks so you can see the ebb and flow of money as a simple transaction for services rendered. At Starbucks, there's a constant exchange of money, and observing that process can be really beneficial for your mindset.

There are some business practices that can make you more comfortable with the idea of taking money, such as:

- Completing the monetary transaction before the service is provided.
- If you're in the middle of a proposal with a potential client, provide a printed invoice. Handing them a paper invoice frees you from having to verbalize the pricing, which can make the process easier.

Taking the money upfront from your client doesn't solve the worthiness issue that often stems from feeling like you shouldn't, but it does strengthen the muscle of moving forward and taking money for your services.

We become entrepreneurs to escape things like control and working for other people, but we create a glass ceiling for ourselves in our business by what we charge.

Often it helps women to think about the impact the money they make can have on their family and their community. Perhaps your income will pay the mortgage, or fund your kid's college, provide for an ailing parent, cover the cost of a dream vacation or allow you to give back to your favorite cause. What would it be like to donate more? The more we make, the more we can create an impact.

You Can't Sell Here

Let's go back to app creator Betsy Furler, who launched the *Your App Lady* business and struggled with not doing her books.

It was very puzzling for me to understand her difficulty in getting new clients for her tech consulting business because she had a thriving speech therapy practice and the most incredible network I have ever seen. Betsy has an unusual capacity to maintain connections with people, and

R.E.S.E.T. Your Mindset

she's lived in the same city her entire life. But she didn't seem comfortable connecting with her network to get more leads for her business.

Originally, she thought her issue was pure money mindset and scarcity. As we dove deeper, she realized it was selling.

Every time she watched a video or talked to her sales coach, she got a queasy feeling in her stomach. That's how she knew there was an issue directly with selling and not wanting to seem salesy. She struggled with this on and off for almost two years, constantly asking herself, *why don't I like to sell?*

One day, Betsy drove by the house that she grew up in, which is not somewhere she goes often or naturally. She stopped—and suddenly a memory hit her.

When she was seven years old, she sold campfire girl candies (a lot like Girl Scout Cookies) through her church where her father was the pastor. After the service one day, when everyone had gathered for coffee hour and the little girls started to sell their candies, one of the church leaders approached Betsy and her Mom.

"Betsy can't sell candy because people might feel obligated to buy from her because of who her father is," they said.

Betsy picked up the message *I am not allowed to sell.*

Other people could sell ... but not her. When I had this conversation with Betsy, whom I had coached for over a year, it's like a light opened up. I had always struggled to fully understand Betsy's barriers—and why she felt so limited to ask her extensive network for help in her business. She always believed there was something wrong with asking people she knew to help her.

Do you see how powerful those roots are?

Since that realization, Betsy worked through her mindset issues and has, to date, 5x'd her rates from two years ago. (Yay Betsy! Way to *raise your rates!*) She has six possible projects in her tech consulting business and a lot of high-level connections that she is now feels confident to ask to help her.

But let's take that memory a bit further.

That memory wasn't just about selling ... it was also about not leveraging her network. Her church was her network! I think the message she picked up was more than not selling, but that she shouldn't sell to those she's connected to in her network. She believed she wasn't allowed to ask those she knew to help her make a connection, buy from her, or work directly with her.

It literally made an immediate difference for her to figure out the root of her issue and the stories she was telling herself. Understanding and awareness brought about a massive change for her.

Your Belief Systems about Money

When I talk to clients about limiting beliefs, we almost always have to discuss money.

Your family, whether that means the family you started or the one you grew up in, has certain beliefs about money that may be positive or negative. No one can escape this fact—all of us have certain cultures around it.

Stop for a moment and think about what your parents said about money while you were growing up. Close your eyes and go back to your childhood if you need to.

What judgments did they put on others regarding money and success?

Did you have a rich relative that divorced their partner and your parents blamed money or success?

Was money a constant source of stress?

Were you given an allowance?

What would happen to your current relationships if you made more than your partner, sibling, or friends?

Those formative years are crucial—we already know this. But what you may not see is that some of those things are impacting our business right now through the limiting money beliefs that they generate.

So how do we work on this?

Let's dig into it.

First thing I want you to do is find the biggest piece of paper you can. A big sketch pad is perfect, but not necessary. A receipt is fine. Whatever you can find, grab it.

Next, you're going to write the word *Money* in the middle of the page and circle it. Send a bunch of lines off that circle like spider legs. Now, I want you to think about the word.

What phrases come to mind?

Write them down. Don't censor them. Don't stop. Whatever words, sentences, judgments, feelings, ideas, or memories come to mind, write them down.

If this isn't working for you, use it like a journal. Free write your thoughts either on the paper or in a document on your computer or in the notes section at the end of this chapter. Brain dump whatever comes to you. Sometimes it's helpful to do it in one sitting so that everything is fresh and moving forward. But do what you can, even if it's in increments.

When you're done with the graph or the journal, take a highlighter and mark negative statements. Study them. What are the underlying implications? What does that particular statement really mean? Do you see a pattern?

Here are a few examples of negative statements about money I hear from clients:

1. Money is the root of all evil.
2. We're not made of money.
3. Money can't buy happiness.
4. Friendship and money are like oil and water.
5. Don't throw good money after bad.
6. Money doesn't grow on trees.
7. We can't afford that.

Now that you have your negative comments highlighted, go through each comment and ask yourself, "Do I agree with this comment now?"

Hopefully the answer is no!

Sometimes, however, there are negative words or beliefs that you agree with—that's okay. Just make a conscious decision so you're not passively incorporating your family or mentor's belief systems. Now, when you don't agree with a negative statement, it's time to reframe it and create a new script in your head.

Go back to your journal or your graph and look at the positive statements about money. Are they really positive statements? Sometimes it may seem like a good belief system, but it's actually a limiting belief.

For example: *don't throw good money after bad.*

This labels money as being good or evil and creates the impression that money can be bad. Money is neither good nor bad, it's neutral. It's a tool.

Reframing

One money phrase that I hear often is: *we can't afford that.*

That is a belief that can really seep into your being because we hear it so often, at all stages of life, and may even think it on a daily basis. Let's tackle that one together. How could you reframe it?

Instead of saying, "We can't afford that," how about adding a more positive twist? Imagine you're at the grocery store and your partner, child, or friend wants to buy an expensive new thing. What do you say?

How about, "Let's make a plan to save for that," or "That wouldn't be a good investment right now, but let's look at next week/month/year."

Can you see how that changes the intent of the phrase?

Another very common limiting belief around money is this: *money doesn't grow on trees.*

This is basically saying that money is not abundant and there's a cap on the amount of money that exists for you. Let's reframe it into something more positive.

"Money is abundant."

"Money comes to me."

"I always have enough to get what I need."

That feels better, doesn't it?

These are the things that our Inner Kind Girl says. Now look back at your negative list. I want you to really dig in to these phrases. Think about what the underlying meanings and intentions. Why do you fear money? Why is it a trigger for you?

Respect Money

Financial advisor and TV host Suze Orman said in her book *The Nine Steps to Financial Freedom*, "Show respect for your money . . . then your money will think and care about you in return."[24]

I read that almost twenty years ago and it has stuck with me ever since.

It's important for women to respect money, which is something I feel we don't represent enough. Per Suze's suggestions in her book, one of the ways you can do that is keeping your cash sorted by denomination and facing the same direction.

Consider it to be a kind of symbol for keeping your money organized, whether that means physically or with your books. (Both home and business.) Showing respect changes your mindset and helps you bring more money into your life.

Is there money floating around your purse or laying around your house?

A great take action step is to gather it all, organize it and deposit it or set it aside to spend.

Are your business books a mess? Take the first step to get them organized today.

In the same vein, interacting with respect to others regarding money is also important. When you receive an invoice, pay it on time.

Do not complain about a client not paying you when you overdue invoices with others.

Respect.

If you're in debt with your personal finances, take steps to get out. I highly recommend Dave Ramsey's program, *Total Money Makeover*. It's often offered through churches—but you don't have to be a church-going person to apply his principles, which are ultimately universal.

Working Hard and Self-Worth

There's a common belief among female entrepreneurs that we have to work really hard—sometimes sacrificing things like family time and health—in order to make six figures or more. Money mindset is often about worthiness.

We may hear thoughts like this in our head: *I am not worthy to receive this amount of money for my time.*

Which is why it's so hard for some women to charge higher rates.

The problem here is that we're co-mingling working hard and worthiness. They're two different things. There's feeling worthy to charge, and then there's feeling that you have to work hard in order to be okay keeping the money.

A lot of women spend more time than necessary working on their business in order to have the perception that they're working "hard". There's often something negative in their past associated with working hard and their worth. They may have been told that *if you work hard then good things can happen*, which leaves the assumption that not working hard means bad things will happen. I have had women share with me that they feel guilty that their business is coming so easily to them—like it's a bad thing.

You don't have to work hard just to work hard! It's not a bad thing if money comes easily.

Sometimes people work hard to stay busy because they're afraid to have time off. They don't know how they'll occupy their mind if they're not working. In that instance, there may be some personal growth they need to do, or work with a therapist to figure out why they need to be constantly busy.

One Final Thought

The power that women have is astounding.

Every day I talk with female entrepreneurs that are changing the world and making the most amazing things happen. When it comes to money, however, we take the shy road. The careful road.

But look at this way: what kind of a difference could you make if you had the money?

The more money women have at their disposal, in their business and personal life, allows for more impact to happen. As a gender, we are more generous. We share all that we have. We give back to communities. We give to our families. Women tend to teach others they know what they're learning—like their children. We are going to give back—getting more money doesn't have to be bad. Money is an enabling power that opens up more opportunity to do good.

Take it from attorney Danielle Liss. "When I allowed myself to think more abundant thoughts, it happened. When I welcomed money, when I decided I want more ... financial comfort ... each time we set the goal, it kept happening."

Now *that* is a money mindset to focus on.

Take Action Solutions

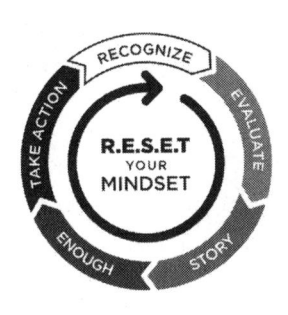

Chapter 11
Take Immediate Action

> "Infuse your life with action. Don't wait for it to happen. Make it happen. Make your own future. Make your own hope. Make your own love."
> —Bradley Whitford, American actor and political activist

What's Next?

We've walked through a lot of real life examples from high-powered female entrepreneurs as they worked through their own mindset issues. By now, the R.E.S.E.T. Framework and the many challenges that you could, do, or will face should be firmly planted in your mind.

Now let's turn to the final step in the framework, *take action*.

Taking action is such a big step that it gets a section all its own.

Once you have gotten to **E—Enough**—and are done being in the place where you are, then it's time to take action.

Many of you know right now what the next action step is in order to move forward on that "thing" you want to make happen. Some of you are still spinning and don't know what to do next.

First, let's break down different ways for you to **take action** because sometimes just having a list to choose from can be a gift.

Taking action may come after you have some self-care time. It may come as soon as you work through the R.E.S.E.T. Framework. Whenever you decide to take action will depend on your experience with this issue, your previous work on mindset issues, and just how overwhelmed you are.

Let's get started with the first steps I take my clients through.

Ways to Take Action

Here are some quick and easy ways to move forward.

- **Braindump.** This is my number one go-to when I'm stuck. With a braindump, there are no rules. You grab a pen and paper, or your laptop and a blank screen, and you write out whatever is bothering you. This can be really enlightening.
- **Exercise.** Not only can the hormone release improve your mood[25], but changing your location and getting out of your chair can put your brain in a different place. Inspiration often comes on the go.
- **Phone a friend.** If you can't work it out on your own, it's time to call in your squad. Starting the conversation with, "I'm having a mindset issue, can you help?" can also cement this for you. Hearing yourself say it—and verbalizing it to others—can be really powerful.
- **Dance it out.** I'm serious. Put on some music and *dance, dance, dance*. Let go. Move to the rhythm. The point is to get out of your current mindset and into something else. It's amazing how letting go will actually help us open up.
- **Power pose.** If you're in the comfort of your own home, or hey, even if you are out in public, take social psychologist Amy Cuddy's advice and strike up a power pose as explained in her viral TedX talk[†] which has been viewed nearly 50 million times. Stand with your arms raised above your head, or your hands on your hips, and feel your own strength. Need some inspiration? Check out this graphic[‡] of awesome power poses from author, powerlifter, and podcaster James Clear.
- **Look at past successes.** This can be particularly powerful if you're stuck in a rut over something new that you're trying or creating, or if you have recently received some difficult feedback. Look back at what you've done well before. Read testimonials or positive emails from former clients and customers. If you're new in your business, this doesn't have to be related. Look at any success, and draw strength from it.

[†] Watch it at https://www.ted.com/talks/amy_cuddy_your_body_language_shapes_who_you_are
[‡] Visit https://jamesclear.com/body-language-how-to-be-confident to see power poses in action.

- **Meditate.** Visualize your goal. Empty your brain. Focus on your breath. Do whatever you have to do to grab a quiet moment; go sink into a different space, and let your mind unwind.
- **Delegate.** Are you putting off something because you really don't want to do it? Delegate it to someone else. If you don't have anyone else, find them. Getting rid of one unwanted task clears up a lot of mental space to keep moving forward.
- **Make a gratitude list.** Write down five things you're grateful for right now. Facing a difficult person or client? Find three things about them that you're grateful for. If you're still feeling stuck or in a negative place, write five more.
- **Take a break.** Walk away from the problem. Walk away from your business. Do something completely unrelated, and come back to it with a fresh mind. Changing locations and activities can work wonders. Need permission? I give it to you right now.
- **Hire a Coach.** Having someone to support you and create accountability and add structure can help you work through roadblocks faster.

How to Take Action

Are you ready to take action, but feeling overwhelmed about where to start? Does the project seem too big?

Let's break it down.

Grab a piece of paper, a pen, or whatever app you use, and list out all the required steps to accomplish the next thing. If you need other resources like software or a contractor or an employee, list that too.

What is the next first step?

This is one of the most important questions you can ask yourself right now. Why? Because the next thing you're going to do is to break it down into smaller pieces. Think of it as a microtask. Often in a project there are several places you can start, so choose one that you most want to do.

If lists aren't your thing—or will make you feel even more overwhelmed and anxious—then this could be a brain dump. Type out everything that comes to your head when you think of what you need to do to tackle a particular issue. If you can get the first thing down, or realize what is your next step, then you're one step closer. This is ideal if you don't know what your next first step is. Just get it out of your mind.

Working through a list or a brain dump is crucial because it takes you out of the paralyzing spin in your head and creates forward momentum. That's what you need most when it comes to taking action.

Here's an example that I've seen before.

Let's say that you have a goal to start putting your name out there as a speaker. To do that, you want to apply at a local event that is right in your niche. The prospect of applying has overwhelmed you. You're experiencing Imposter Syndrome, fear of failure, and possibly more. After using the R.E.S.E.T. Framework to transform your fears, you realize it's time to do something.

This is the most exciting part!

Finally, you're at the **take action** step. Let's breakdown a possible first step for applying to this speaking opportunity.

1. Fill out the application on the website.

Does that feel too big right now? Sometimes applications or pitches involve multiple steps and are small projects on their own. Maybe the idea of it overwhelms you because you know it will take hours to finalize. It's okay. We can break this task down farther into microtasks that will feel less daunting.

1. Fill out the application on the website.
   1.1 Create profile on website
   1.2 Upload your headshot
   1.3 Load resume
2. Review resume
   2.1 Have friend check it for errors
   2.2 Give overview of topic
3. Provide references
   3.1 Reach out to three people for a reference letter

My guess is that you have the time, or ability, at that moment to open the browser, input your email and password, and create your profile for that application. Task 1.1—DONE! While you're at it, why don't you upload your profile picture (remember a good enough picture works, don't delay applying until you get professional headshots done or redone)? Task 1.2—DONE! Be sure to cross those off if you've made a list.

Feels better, doesn't it?

You may not need to microtask to that level—that's totally fine. This is where your self-awareness comes into play. **What will be best for you?** What is going to motivate you to greater action?

I've found that after doing that little thing, most women decide that it wasn't so bad, and they're spurred on with greater excitement to do other things. Allowing small parts to create a whole is a powerful way to move through the paralysis of work that has mindset issues associated with it.

You'll find yourself saying, *okay, that was easy. Now what else can I do?*

Are you still feeling stuck or overwhelmed with doing that next first thing? No problem, there's a solution for that.

5, 4, 3, 2, 1 it!

It's time to implement the Five Second Rule, made popular by author Mel Robbins.

This is a favorite strategy of attorney Danielle Liss. She uses it all the time to move from procrastination to action, and she shared it with me and the other women in her mastermind. We all started using it with great results.

The idea is to count backwards from five. When you get to one, you "blast off" and do the next first step you have decided on.

You don't think about whether or not you should, you just do it.

How did Mel come up with this means of moving people to action?

A number of years ago, Mel found herself in a terrible rut. She was staying up late, drinking a lot, and then when the morning came, she would ignore her alarm and end up sleeping late. Then she would be frustrated she was getting a late start on the day and beat herself up (that Inner Mean Girl knows no bounds). At the end of the day, she would feel so deflated that she self-soothed with alcohol.

The next day would be a tragic repeat.

Until she had **enough**.

A rocket on TV inspired her one night. She decided the next morning to break her pattern and launch herself out of bed. When her alarm went off, she would 5-4-3-2-1 in her mind and get up. She wouldn't think, she'd just *do*.

To her surprise ... it worked.

She has been 5-4-3-2-1-ing her life ever since and is a highly sought after and top paid speaker.

Why does this work?

Well, it taps into the research we have previously discussed about our evolutionary brain trying to protect us from harm. Our brain thinks that things that make us uncomfortable might not keep us "safe".

Our action steps for our businesses are not endangering our physical bodies, so we just need to do them. That old lizard brain really needs to evolve and catch up with the times!

One of the best parts of the Five Second Rule is that Mel didn't intend for it to become an international phenomenon, or propel her to the top paid stages in the world.

It was an aside mentioned in the last two minutes of her 2011 TED Talk[†] titled *Stop Screwing Yourself Over.*

Her TED talk has over thirteen million views. Her book *The Five Second Rule* is an international bestseller with numerous testimonials from readers who have used it to transform their lives and take action.

Let's dive into a few examples that you may relate to.

1. When you look at your inbox, and you see **534 unread messages** staring at you, and you hesitate because you don't even want to start, that's when you count. Then you put your hand on the mouse, and click on the first one.
2. You're staring at a list of client prospects that you're afraid to call because you don't want to bother them. That's when you count backward; then pick up the phone, and dial the first one before you kill the idea.
3. There's an idea for a new product that you really want to create and launch, but it's a huge risk, and you aren't sure it'll be effective. You count backward, then you start.
4. You have a huge goal that you want to work toward, but it seems far too big, too grand, for you to even write down. Count backward, and write it down.

The remarkable thing here is that through counting backward, we're stopping our usual mental processes and silencing our Inner Mean Girl. We're moving past our fears. By counting backward (it doesn't

---

[†] Listen to it at https://www.ted.com/talks/mel_robbins_how_to_stop_screwing_yourself_over.

work the same if you count from one to five), you stop the downward spiral in your mind and leap into action.

That's what you need. It's why you're here reading this book right now.

Are you ready to get unstuck? Use the next page to move yourself to action.

Go Take Some Action!

Write 3 methods that help you take action.

1.

2.

3.

Chapter 12
Self-Care

> "Almost everything will work again if you unplug it for a few minutes, including you."
>
> —*Anne Lamott, novelist and political activist*

Every time I'm on an airplane, they make a safety announcement to put your own oxygen mask on first before you help a child or someone else.

The idea feels counterintuitive.

I have to mentally remind myself each flight that, in the event of an emergency, I must take care of myself before I help my family. The idea of not helping my children first flies in the face of every maternal instinct in my body.

So I have to remind myself as I sit on the tarmac, watching the flight attendants role play how to put on an air mask, that if I don't get my own mask on, I might pass out from lack of oxygen before I can help my kids.

The truth is, I need to remind myself of this every day.

Not in terms of air masks and oxygen, but in terms of setting aside time for me. You know what I mean. Taking time to take care of my body and give it the healthy food it needs and the movement and rest it desires, for example.

Every morning, I imagine a helpful flight attendant reminding me to set aside time for a walk and a lunch break—not lunch in front of my laptop!

Women are socialized to constantly put everyone's needs ahead of our own. But if we don't take care of ourselves, it impacts everything! Our relationships, our health, our home, and our happiness. We're living in a culture that esteems being overscheduled and values "busyness".

In this chapter, we're going to talk about ways to slow down and take care of yourself so that you can take care of others—whether that means your clients, your family, your friends, or anyone else. Many women I work with tell me they feel guilty taking time for self care. They seem to think there's only enough time for work or family, but we MUST take time for our own well-being. The compounding effect of not putting your "oxygen mask on first" results in a worn down, tense, tired, grumpy, out-of-shape woman.

That is certainly not something I am aspiring to.

So let's dive deeper into self-care and why not doing it could be sabotaging your mindset.

What is Self-Care?

All you have to do is type *self-care* into a search engine, and countless responses populate—blog posts on how to do it, what it means, when to do it, and what works. Here's the truth about self-care: it's individual.

It boils down to one thing: **self-care is an action you take that fills you up and doesn't drain you.**

Notice how I said *action*?

Throughout my business, I've noticed an unfortunate truth: a lot of women discount the importance of self-care. That's crazy! It's one of the most powerful tools in our belt.

In fact, studies have shown that being mindful about your stress levels—and attempting to reduce them—helps us cope better. That includes self-care strategies like yoga and meditation (which we'll get into more later).

Men vs. Women

Men are wired differently than women. They also run businesses and homes differently than women.

In fact, a study[26] that appeared in Harvard Business Review found that men are more likely to view a leadership position as a transactional position with subordinates, and women are more focused on interactive leadership, with encouragement, energy, and charisma.

We naturally put more of ourselves into our work while trying to maintain a large role in household duties.

In other words, men are able to block home, life, dinner, daycare, and other things out of their mind more easily than women. It's true! They compartmentalize while we try to keep all the balls in the air and multitask home and business responsibilities. Many of my clients work from home and can easily fill their days alternating through household chores, business duties, and family errands.

Instead of being single-minded, we feel as if we're pulled everywhere. Couple that with never taking time for yourself, and you're heading for a meltdown.

Running a business is a marathon, not a sprint, and we need to make sure we have enough energy for the duration.

Where to Start

The following are a few suggestions that I have created based on my client work. These will help you take care of yourself so that you can stop self-sabotaging—and then take care of everyone else.

Note: this is NOT just for Moms! This is a section that is focused on any woman that gets immersed into their businesses or lives or family—whether you have children or not.

A shout out to my Mom, who taught me all these lessons through modeling and being a prime example of self-care.

—Take Care of Your Body—

If you don't feel good, you're not going to work as productively, efficiently, or with the same enthusiasm. This can mean many things: working out, eating the right food, getting enough sleep, regular visits with your doctor, or taking a break when you're sick. Yes. I said it. You need to take time off if you're sick!

—Maintain Your Friendships—

There's no feeling quite so hollow as when you look around and realize that all your friends are online. This is definitely personal experience speaking. There have been times in my life when I've hunkered into my business and haven't connected in person. You can be surrounded by people and still feel lonely.

It is not a good feeling.

In this regard, consider something you may not have considered before (introverts—I'm looking at you!): the power of in-person events is undeniable and a great way to make new friends.

Even if your friends have nothing to do with your business space, which may be a good idea, it's okay to schedule, plan, and make time for friendships. Remove the guilt from taking time away from your business so you can maintain important friendships.

If you have kids, play groups make it super simple. You can meet at a park; the kids play while you talk; and you don't even have to find childcare! It's a double bonus if the other mom's are also entrepreneurs.

Get out. Be with people.

—Date Your Partner—

Our relationships are a priority! I know how hard it is to plan time together and make it happen, especially when you throw multiple careers, exponential growth, and other family members into the process. Finding childcare, figuring out events, dinners—any of those issues can make it very challenging. But the rewards outweigh the effort.

I promise.

Not only do you take a step away from the business and clear your mind when you actually date your partner, but it gives you some definitive one-on-one time with the most important person in your life.

Don't feel like you have to dive in fully right away. It can be hard to make a weekly date—so go for a monthly date. Then shift it to twice a month. When it's easier, or you're more in the groove, try the weekly date. You don't have to have a big dinner date every time. Work out together. Go to lunch together. Shop for groceries.

It may require some creativity, but it will pay itself out. You're an entrepreneur. Challenge is where you thrive!

—Hire Help—

Do you need permission to hire someone to help you get things done—or clear the way for you to take care of yourself? I'm giving it to you.

You are worthy to have help in your home.

Here's a quick list of help that you can hire:

1. Babysitters
2. Housekeeper
3. Yard work
4. Driver for kids/errands
5. Grocery shopping
6. Cook

—Pamper Yourself—

You should absolutely pamper yourself.

Don't wait until things look really bad to make a grooming appointment (believe me, I've been there). You're worth consistent pampering. Again, this is something that you may not allow to happen organically, so plan your self-care in advance—sometimes I schedule it out months ahead of time.

Call the hair stylist or nail salon, and actually book your time slot. That will hold you to it.

Who wouldn't love a mani-pedi once a month?

—Don't Forget Your Hobbies—

Not only will this keep your creative juices flowing for your business, but getting your mind on something else can help your subconscious work more efficiently on obstacles that you're facing. Focusing solely on one area of your life can dry you out.

It's time to reach broader.

—Take Time to Look Nice—

In other words: take care of yourself first!

No, you don't have to wear heels and lipstick every day. This shouldn't be a stressful self-care mechanism. But how good does it feel to take a few minutes every day, in the morning, to just get ready and prepared for the day? I can guarantee it can be the dividing point between good and bad days.

Do you have little kids? I understand how hard it can be to get going in the morning. They're up all night long, have early hours, and you may be exhausted just from taking care of them the day before. But I really believe that this is the most important time to start caring for yourself in the morning.

Give yourself a minimum of eight minutes every day. If you need to, take this as a challenge—set the timer, and see how it affects the rest of your day. Eight minutes gives you time to wash your face, brush your teeth, throw on some makeup, put your hair up, and get started on the day.

I know you can spare eight minutes. If you have more time, go for it. I usually spend about thirty minutes getting ready in the morning while I listen to a podcast.

When my brother and I were little, my mom used to lock us in the bathroom with her when she showered so we'd be safe. (I remember trying to figure out how to unlock the door and escape!) She took that time to look and feel good about herself.

It's time all of us do the same.

Self-Protection

One thing I end up talking to people about is the concept of protecting themselves from people or situations that make them feel less than. This can include people in your life that are not supportive, or some influencers or peers on social media whose posts trigger you.

Social media is a double-edged sword. It's a wonderful connecting and advertising ground, especially for businesses of any size. But it can also be addicting, demotivating, and problematic for relationships and real-life interaction. That's a breeding ground for mindset issues.

Which is why I say this all the time: care enough about you and your mental state to protect yourself.

Sometimes that means you have to unfollow people on social media, unsubscribe from email lists, or take a break from platforms for a while. It might mean skipping an event, changing the subject on a conversation, or setting a boundary with a close friend.

Do it.

I give you permission to love people but not allow them to impact your mindset.

I give you permission to admire lots of people, but not be on their email list.

I even give you permission to stop following me if you find my content, or me, to be a trigger for you. Don't put yourself there.

Protect your mindset.

Keep in mind that there are times when we're more vulnerable to mindset issues. If I'm in creation mode, I try not to look at anyone else's content. I don't want to be burdened by worrying about what others are saying or doing and whether I measure up. Call it creative protection mode or whatever you want, but it's one of the biggest ways I take care of myself.

And don't forget about that lovely monthly cycle we all go through. If you track your period, you may find that mindset issues crop up with greater intensity around that time.

This section leads directly into my next point.

What You See May Not Be Real

Something interesting that I've noticed is that we put a lot of romantic ideas into the people that we're watching. We follow people on social media or keep track of our peers and build up a picture in our head of what their life and businesses must look like.

"They're so far ahead of me," we might think. Another that I hear is, "I don't know how she does it. She literally does *everything*. And she does it so well! She must be making tons of money on her new launch/product/business."

My cautionary advice: what you see may not be real ... or at least may not be the entire picture.

Can we stop comparing the messy insides of our life to someone else's highlight reel?

The cropped pictures on social media are my favorite. Sort through Instagram or Twitter or Facebook, and it shouldn't take you too long to find one. Now think about what you might see if you were to pull back the view.

Their house in shambles, maybe?

A child crying on the floor?

Dishes overflowing in the sink?

Maybe their house would be pristine, but it wouldn't reflect the three hours it took to clean it or the hassle of keeping the kids out. Or the thousands of attempts at perfecting one recipe. Or the hours of sorting through photos and editing them to get just the right look.

We rarely see the mess.

We don't really know what's going on in someone else's business, or their bank account. The perception of wealth based on a photo of their immaculate kitchen may have actually come through a bunch of discount stores. Or ten years of really hard work and dogged determination.

Or not much money at all.

No one has it all figured out. That's okay! You can still be successful and have a messy back-end to your business. Stop comparing yourself to everyone else. I call it *comparing our insides to everyone else's outsides*. It doesn't work.

Guess what? I'm a mess too. So, stop comparing, and grant yourself that peace of mind.

Can you do that?

Can you stop comparing?

Can you stop creating fantasies that the other business owner has it all figured out? Or balances everything? Or has a ginormous bank account?

To help you feel better, here is a list—that isn't comprehensive—of things I've observed female entrepreneurs struggle with:

- Saying 'no'
- Feeling unorganized
- Difficulty with personal relationships
- Scared of her own big dreams
- Hiring
- Unworthiness
- Email management
- Client boundaries
- Taking risks
- Processes
- Systems
- Technology
- Organization
- Conquering fears
- Trouble focusing
- Onboarding
- Beating herself up
- Not fitting in

Do any of the above describe your struggles right now? No matter what story you've created in your head about that other person, stop using it to compare your business to theirs. Not comparing is protective, more efficient, and gives a lot less access to our Inner Mean Girl who always wants to tear us down.

Also, keep in mind that just because someone else has a professional photo session smacked all over their social media, doesn't mean that their everyday life looks like a perfect Instagram account.

By comparing, we're setting dangerous expectations that we cannot maintain. Be really careful about the expectations we create for ourselves, because we often put the most pressure on.

That is not self-care.

It will not profit your business, your family, your health, or your life.

A Few More

Just in case the above wasn't enough to get your juices flowing, I reached out to women in my Facebook group, The BizChix Coop, to see what they did for self-care. Here are some of their responses. Find one or two you like; then go take some action!

- Early morning workouts are a must.
- Organizing something—it calms me down.
- Spooning my dog. He's so warm!
- I have my hair blown out twice a week. It chills me.
- Diffusing essential oils.
- Chai tea!
- Watching cooking shows in the morning.
- Go out for a solo lunch.
- Retail therapy!
- Reading fiction.
- Booking myself an extra night at a business event.
- Taking a three hour nap.
- Taking Saturdays off completely.
- Social-media-free day once a week.
- Knitting.
- Doing jigsaw puzzles.
- Saturday mornings are for Mommy!
- Family days.
- Laughing with friends.
- Sunday is meal prep for the week.
- Getting out of my head by hiking/walking/yoga.

If you've been waiting for someone to give you permission to take care of yourself, let me be the first to say, "Permission Granted".

Go Take Some Action!

Write 1-3 ways you want to focus on taking better care of yourself.

1.

2.

3.

Chapter 13
Affirmations

> *"Affirmations are our mental vitamins, providing the supplementary positive thoughts we need to balance the barrage of negative events and thoughts we experience daily."*
> —Tia Walker, blogger and founder of A-List Diet and Fitness

Our mind is continuously meditating on thoughts. So why not take control and choose positive statements instead of negative or self-deprecating thoughts? Affirmations, for example, are positive statements about the future that you repeat to yourself.

When it comes to affirmations, it seems there are two camps: they work, and they don't work.

There are arguments for both sides. Psychologist Suzanne Gelb believes they work—but only when undertaken with intense honesty. The reason I bring this up?

They're powerful and I have watched them change my clients and my own mindset.

If you find you have deeper, underlying issues to root out in order to help the affirmations do their job, that's an action step I highly urge you to take. Before we dive into this little miracle worker, let's talk about the power of positive thought.

The Power of Positivity

We've already discussed that the Inner Mean Girl puts thoughts in your head that are less than charitable—and finally noticing those is the first step to correcting them. But there are other ways that we can impact the scripts in our head.

The power of positive thinking.

In other words, channel that Inner Kind Girl.

To say that there's a movement out there to emphasize this fact would be an understatement. There are entire bodies of work on positive self-talk—not to mention studies to prove that it works—that can help you find, change, and move through those scripts that pop up and lead to self-sabotaging.

For example, one study found that positive thinking underlies life satisfaction, self-esteem, and optimism[27]. A different study of women attempting to lose weight showed that optimistic expectations yielded better results[28]. Another study showed the importance of positive thoughts in depression relapse and recovery[29].

There's more where that came from.

Thinking positively is something I've been working on my whole life. Thanks to years of practice, I can work through mindset issues fairly quickly these days. I attribute much of my success to positive thinking and training my mind to stay positive.

Over time, I've experienced (and seen first hand in other female entrepreneurs) that remaining bitter and negative about ourselves, our life situation, or our struggles isn't helpful.

In fact, it can move us backward.

Meet Tara

Writing about affirmations without including my client, Tara Humphrey, would be a disservice to you.

Tara runs a multi-six-figure project management and consultancy business outside of London. Her work has impacted over 5.7 million patients. She is one of the most high functioning people that I know—managing three kids, a CEO position at her company, a very intense exercise regime (think ultramarathon treks), and she is working toward earning her Ph.D.

She does it with the power of affirmations.

Before she started her own business, she worked as a business development manager at a University. Unfortunately, she hated her position. One day her sister said to her, "Don't focus on where you are now. Focus on where you want to be." Tara had a designer notebook given to her as a gift. She thought, *I'm going to start writing down how I want to feel.*

So she did.

She wrote things like: *I'm going to have a really good day today,* or *my boss and I are going to have such a laugh. The next time I speak at a meeting, everybody is really going to like my idea.*

Sometimes she would write the same thing over and over again. Such as *I'm going to be the CEO of a healthcare organization.* She went out and bought a jumper and put the letters CEO on it. She'd wear it every night so she could see the letters. She'd write that same affirmation down every night.

I am going to be a CEO of a healthcare organization.

Four years later, she has twenty notebooks filled up. She is now the CEO of her own healthcare organization—and it is skyrocketing.

Creating Opportunities

One of the amazing things about Tara and her affirmations is how she's truly created opportunity for herself through his method. With full confidence, she can say that she's attracted every opportunity she's had.

> "I just assume it's going to happen, or I figure out how to make it happen."

She told me that creating opportunity through affirmations was like creating her business. One step at a time. A recent experience of hers struck me as fascinating.

A relatively small client came to her business and created a very uncomfortable situation. They would only negotiate over email, would not take her calls, and made everything more difficult than it needed to be. She didn't want to be in the situation of haggling over price and minute details again, so she made the affirmation, *I secure multiple six-figure contracts, no questions asked.*

A week later, she secured a six-figure contract.

No questions asked.

To foreshadow our next chapter, Tara also created a vision board. On it, she placed a picture of a graduation hat at the bottom that said *with distinction.*

She graduated with her MBA with distinction.

Make Them Work

That's great it works for Tara, I imagine you may be thinking, *but how can I make it work for me and my business?*

Great question. Here are a few ideas for how to incorporate affirmations into a business sphere.

1. At her office, Tara places a weekly affirmation on a whiteboard for her team to see.
2. She gifted each team member with a Five Minute Journal that they write in each morning. They list three things they're grateful for, what would make that day great, and a daily affirmation. In the evening, they write three things that made the day amazing and what could have been done better.
3. She posts affirmation signs throughout her office.
4. The number of affirmations (and the affirmations themselves) depend on the day and what it requires. Don't be afraid to change that around.
5. Before a looming meeting, conversation, or other event, she writes out *how will I have an excellent meeting today?* Then she decides! She makes a plan of action. (I love women that epitomize my favorite catch phrase—go take some action!) For example, she may write, *I will pack my bag the night before. I will check if my car needs gas so I don't have to do it in the morning. I will choose my clothes and have them ready.* This is applicable on all levels of business—particularly if you have partners or employees—to help you stay on the same page.

Eight Quick Tips to Get Started

Tara has been doing this affirmation work for four years now. It's infused into her thought life and part of her daily practice. We can all get there too—it's just a matter of starting.

Here are eight quick tips to get you started.

1. **Be specific.** If you're not specific, the universe can't give it to you. For example, if you say, "I want a contract," then you could get anything. "I want a six-figure contract," is much more specific.

2. **Be creative with how you take the affirmations in.** Say them in the mirror. Better yet, write one on the mirror every day or every week with a dry-erase marker. Keep that marker in the bathroom so it's ready. Create a background for your computer. Record them on your phone, and play them back to yourself while you drive around. Use sticky notes on your car dash.
3. **Don't be attached to how the affirmations come to fruition.** Tara is the CEO of a healthcare organization, but it wasn't the one, or the way, she expected. She imagined she'd be headhunted by NHS England instead of owning her own business. (Which could still happen.)
4. **You don't need a fancy notepad.** Put them in your phone, or text them to yourself. Write them on the back of a receipt. Keep a pile of scratch paper handy.
5. **Don't overthink it.** Just write down what would make you happy that day. How do you want to feel? What do you want from the day? It could be getting an ice cream or making a phone call. Once you decide, make it a game. What can you get this day? This week? This month?
6. **Focus on what you want to feel.** Regardless of how ridiculous or silly it seems. Write it down for you. No one else is going to see it.

List of Affirmations

It would be remiss of me to leave you with all this great direction, but no affirmations to start with. (You can always make your own, of course!)

Tara isn't my only client that uses the power of affirmations in her business. Remember Goldi, the chiropractor that wouldn't pay herself more than her husband made? She also keeps an affirmation journal. In fact, she shares affirmations with her mom, and they often discuss their power.

Here are some affirmations that Goldi shared with me:

I excel at making money.

I'm a good businessperson.

I make decisive decisions.

I am rich.

I can afford all the things and experiences required for me to live a happy, healthy, abundant lifestyle.

Money represents security and freedom for my family.

Money is a tool that provides a roof over our heads, comfort, freedom, food, and flexibility for expenses and experiences for my family and friends.

Here are a few of Tara's favorite affirmations.

My risks pay off.
I am not frightened to walk away.
I live without fear.
I always learn and never fail.
I trust my instinct; it never fails me.
I have the time, capacity, and resources to achieve my goals.
Money flows to me in abundance.
I choose not to focus on money. Why would I when I already have it?

Here is my favorite affirmation right now.

Everything works out for me.

What are three affirmations that would help you in your life right now?

Go Take Some Action!

Write 1-3 affirmations you could say to yourself today.

1.

2.

3.

Chapter 14
Visualization

> *"Visualize this thing that you want. See it, feel it, believe in it. Make your mental blueprint, and begin to build."*
> —*Robert Collier, self-help and new thought author*

Call it manifesting, vision-casting, meditating, picturing, day-dreaming, or whatever you want; visualization is one of the most powerful tools you have in your pocket as an entrepreneur. And, sadly, one of the most underutilized.

Let's talk about this powerhouse.

The Power of Seeing It in Your Mind

When I was a young swimmer, I learned visualization to help with swimming competitions.

A sports psychologist came to the sleep-away swimming camp I attended during middle school and taught us how to get into a really relaxed physical state and then visualize our success. He had us visualize our race from start to finish. Completing any pre-race rituals. Even little things, like putting on my cap and goggles. Feeling the water lap around my shoulders as I realized a perfect start. Every detail of the race going just as I wanted it to go. Swimming down the middle of the lane. A fantastic turn. Other swimmers struggling to keep up. Seeing the exact time I wanted at the very end.

Guess what?

It worked.

That was a powerful tool to learn at a very young age and one that has served me well throughout all my life, but especially as an entrepreneur.

Visualization in Action

In order to prepare for my first live event, BizChix Live, I sat down, envisioned my goals, and vision-casted many parts of it. For example, I focused on giving a successful keynote address. Mingling during the yacht ride.

But above all—I vision-casted the final toast.

In my minds eye, I pictured myself at the end of BizChix Live. The buzz in my veins from such a phenomenal event. The feel of the champagne glass in my hand. All the faces of those in front of me. In my vision-casting, I could feel my own success—and how sweet it was! From the beginning, I visualized and craved that moment.

Guess what?

It happened.

In fact, that moment was bigger than what I could have ever vision-casted. It was more than I could have imagined. While standing in front of those women, representing female entrepreneurs and other women that were just like me, I came back to myself.

I remembered who I was and what I was capable of.

My ex-husband's affair affected me deeply and in more ways than one. Despite picking up the pieces and marrying a wonderful man, growing a successful online business, and having three beautiful children, that was the moment I felt like myself again. Like the Natalie that had existed before the affair.

Before the humiliation and divorce.

I was back.

Psychocybernetics

Maxwell Maltz started out as a plastic surgeon.

After many surgeries, he noticed a trend in his patients after recovery. Some of them underwent surgery and went on to a better, happier life. The others received the change, then remained stuck as if the surgery had never been performed.

This strange phenomenon launched him on an exploration of psychology that would eventually change his practice, his life, and the lives of the millions of people that have bought or read his book, *Psychocybernetics*.[30]

In *Psychocybernetics*, Maltz poses the idea that our brains are like a computer. Whatever data we feed ourselves is the data it will process. He refers to it as the input. For example, *I'm so nervous; I know I'm going to botch this interview.* The data you're giving yourself is, *I am going to botch this interview.* Because that's in your mind, that's your focus.

That's what you will create.

If you fed your brain the idea, *I am going into this interview with confidence in my ability to do this job,* then that's the data it will process.

That's what you will create.

As part of his book, one of the most important things he recommends to each person is visualization. He refers to it as both *creative mental picturing* and *visualization.* He instructs the following: "The method to be used consists of creative mental picturing, creatively experiencing through your imagination, and the formation of new automatic reaction patterns by 'acting out' and 'acting as if.'"

In other words: Use visualization to experience your goal and create the situation *as if* it were happening right then. Visualize your goal.

The way I did with BizChix Live.

In visualizing our goals, we are telling our brains, *this is where I want to go.* Our subconscious then knows what to do because of the data you have, or are, giving it. That means we'll make better decisions to steer ourselves that way.

In later chapters, Maltz also counsels that thinking in terms of the end result—or me holding champagne at the end of BizChix Live—is giving your brain the data it needs. Don't think about the how. Think about the *what.* What do you want? What can you visualize in deep clarity and detail? As soon as your brain has that input, the how will unfold. It will come to you.

The power of this is unbelievable.

The Reticular Activating System

For those of you that like to understand things on a deeper level, let's get into some anatomy. The Reticular Activating System (RAS) is a bundle of neurons in our brain stem that influences our behaviors. It helps us create and manifest our intentions. It filters out unnecessary information to prevent us from getting overwhelmed by the data and stimuli around us. When we're interested or focusing on something, it looks for data and inputs to support that.

This is what is behind the power of affirmations and visualization.

R.E.S.E.T. Your Mindset

If we are constantly focusing on negative thoughts our outcomes, the RAS will work to make that come true.

The opposite is true as well.

When we focus on positive thoughts and outcomes, our brain provides support for those things and helps those things to come true.

More Votes for Visualization

Here are some other well-known people that have used visualization to achieve incredible results.

1. **Jim Carrey**[31] : This comedian and actor is more than just a funny guy. He credits much of his success to using visualization. One of his visualization success stories goes back to 1985 when, as a struggling actor, he wrote himself a $10 million check for "acting services rendered" and dated it ten years in the future (Thanksgiving, 1995) and kept it in his wallet. Just before Thanksgiving 1995, he found out he was going to make $10 million for the film *Dumb and Dumber*.
2. **Alex Honnold**[32] : He's the only person to have solo-climbed El Capitan in Yosemite National Park. He visualized it for months—if not years—before doing something most deemed impossible.
3. **Michael Phelps**[33] : Phelps's coach, Bob Bowman, had Phelps practice three things every day to become a champion. The first one? Visualization. The second? Mental practice.
4. **Arnold Schwarzenegger**: When asked about his work as a bodybuilder, Schwarzenegger said, "I had this fixed idea of growing a body like Reg Park's. The model was there in my mind; I only had to grow enough to fill it. The more I focused in on this image and worked and grew, the more I saw it was real and possible for me to be like him."

And finally, let's revisit Tara Humphrey again.

When she has a big meeting or event coming up, she visualizes a successful meeting. Sometimes she records how she imagines the meeting will go on her phone and plays it back while brushing her teeth, driving, or she'll fall asleep listening to it. The moment she wakes up?

She's picturing that successful meeting. She anticipates how she'll react if they say something she doesn't like, or what she'll say, or how to meet obstacles head on. She'll even create affirmations around how she wants to feel after the meeting.

I love this for so many reasons, but specifically because she's taking action in so many creative ways.

For me, writing this book has been a huge challenge. I love the idea of helping others with their mindset, spreading success stories, and sharing my experiences and the R.E.S.E.T. Framework. But there were also so many decisions to make, and I really dislike the editing process.

Visualizing the book being done and holding it in my hands has kept me going.

I imagine what it will be like to hand it to my husband and teen daughter. I imagine being at my live event and surprising all the women in the audience with their first print edition. I imagine the pride on my parents' face when they get their first copy. I will be the first person in my family to write a book!

Visualization is powerful. It can help you accomplish goals that might seem improbable or even impossible.

Now think about the next big thing you want to accomplish.

Focus on the final moment of completion. What will it feel like? Where will you be? What will you be wearing? Who else will be there? What other details can you map out to help make the moment more real in your mind?

Go Take Some Action!

What are three things you can visualize succeeding at? Try choosing something to visualize that you want to happen in the next day, the next week, and the next month.

1.

2.

3.

Chapter 15
Gratitude

> "Gratitude makes sense of our past, brings peace for today, and creates a vision for tomorrow."
> —Melody Beattie, author of bestselling novel Codependent No More

Let's take a breath and be grateful. Especially for our businesses. We have a lot. We have the opportunity to be business owners, to manage our own destiny, and to lead our own teams. Some of us can work from home, pick our own clients, and reach beyond our hometowns. We are transforming their future.

Gratitude is well-documented as one of the most powerful ways to change your life and cultivate positive thinking. There's a reason that productivity journals include daily and weekly slots for things you are grateful for.

In fact gratitude (and visualizing our best possible self) have proven to increase and maintain our mood positively, especially as continued over time. And it compounds over time. In one study, three separate groups of people were assigned to either a daily or weekly gratitude lists (the control group was not). Those who expressed gratitude showed heightened well-being, supporting the idea that consciously focusing on our blessings has emotional and interpersonal benefits.

The pastor at my church in California has given us the same message every Sunday before Thanksgiving for many years. Why? Because the entire congregation wants it. Some people have even memorized what he says and demand that he gives it every year following. Having heard it many times, I can tell you that it's a powerful message. One I want to share with you.

He defines thankfulness in a way that causes me to think about it all year long. His message is universal.

Wanting What You Have

My pastor defines gratitude or thankfulness as *wanting what you have*.

For example, it means you can wake up, know your hair is a mess, and can think, *I want this hair. It couldn't be better.*

Could it? Maybe. Probably. Morning hair isn't exactly styled and prepared to go into the world. But being content with what you have in the moment is a powerful, powerful thing.

Why?

Because you're not constantly peering over the fence, trying to find what's better that you don't have.

Let's put this into action. Find something in your life that stands out to you right this minute.

This could be really simple and could be literally anything. Want something challenging?

Look in the mirror.

Then you're going to say this: *I want/love* (whatever you're looking at). *It couldn't be better. I love my body, it couldn't be any better. I love my closet, it couldn't be any better. I love my partner, they couldn't be any better.*

It's pretty great to wake up and even *have* hair, right?

This may not feel natural at first. It may feel like a naive, false approach to life. Trust me: it gets easier.

Love Your Business

Now let's step back and apply this to your business. Stick with me here and say this out loud: I love my business; it couldn't be better.

Did you stutter? Did you stumble? Was there a ... *but* ... that came onto the end? Don't worry. It happens to me too. This is what I want to help you release—those negative thoughts that creep in. We give them power. A lot of power. So, for this moment, I want you to allow that positive statement to really just sink in. No *buts*. No clarifications. No lists of things that could be so much better.

I love my business; it couldn't be better.

Do you feel a difference?

Acknowledging contentment allows you to be fully present in your gratitude. It doesn't mean that you have no plans for improvement, or things to do, or ideas to enact. You have appreciation right now. That's powerful.

Gratitude removes us from a place of comparison. It takes away the power of the negative mindset and puts us in a feeling of being enough. It also removes anxiety and panic that can tangle us in our own thoughts and help us self-sabotage.

We are business owners. We have power over our lives, over our future, over our business (even when it may not feel like it.)

For me, I am grateful to do quality, amazing work with women around the world without having to leave the comfort of my home.

Remember, you are in a place that could not be any better. Now, repeat that to yourself, and let it take you higher.

Celebrating Your Wins

For this reason, all of my masterminds and client calls start with having them recount a recent win in their life. Remembering them and saying them out loud calls back to mind the good things that happen. It's a reminder to be thankful for what we have.

There are plenty of times when someone says to me that they can't find anything good that happened. When we dig a little deeper, there is always something that was a win. Keep in mind that there is no size requirement here; no win has to be big. Wins are not massive triumphs all the time. Sometimes it's just a win that we got out of bed, right?

You can start the day on a win simply because the day began. We're alive. Breath fills our lungs. We have creative space in our minds. Even the worst days still mean that we're alive. Something good can be found out of every situation.

What I often find is that a recent negative experience overshadows a huge win in my client's previous week. They will completely erase the win from their mind and focus only on the negative. There is that lizard brain trying to protect us again! Try creating a weekly practice of writing down at least one win.

Skewing Negative

Our brains are wired to think negatively.

You can have a lot of experiences telling you that you are good enough, your business is successful, and things are going well ... but we always skew negative. Our brain has been proven to have a negative bias[34], even when inputting positive events. In fact, it's so sensitive, we skew negative at the earliest stage of information processing. It's fight or flight. Paying attention to negative experiences keep us safe.

Licensed Marriage and Family Therapist, Amber Hawley and I have discussed this penchant of our brain to skew negative[†]. "What we focus on expands," she told me. It's the same principle that Maxwell Maltz discussed in *Psychocybernetics*.

What if these are your thoughts? *All my clients are going to leave me. This is a really bad month. I'll never make enough money. My clients are dissatisfied; I can tell.*

You're so busy worrying that it becomes a self-fulfilling prophecy. You're sabotaging yourself because you're only thinking about the negative and not doing the things that are functional and helpful.

Now say your wins out loud. Speak your gratitude.

I'm grateful I have clients to work with. Money flows to me easily. My husband and I have smooth communication, and I'm grateful we can talk about my fears tonight.

Sounds a lot like affirmations, doesn't it?

I've said it before: our inner thought life is all connected and impacts our daily life and accomplishments.

When we say our wins out loud, they stay with us. This is just one way to counter our evolutionary negative skew. Our brains are trying to keep us safe, to protect us from any type of pain or discomfort, but that doesn't mean they have to rule our lives.

Meditation

Many of you have tried—or at least heard of—the power of meditation. In fact, meditation used in combination with gratitude is a powerful force. Meditation has been known to increase gratitude, compassion, and an overall sense of well-being.

Let's visit attorney Danielle Liss again.

While undergoing her journey through mindset issues, Danielle stumbled on the book *You Have Four Minutes to Change Your Life* by Rebekah Borucki.[35]

---

† If you want to learn more about this negative bias, or about Amber's work with high-performing couples, get the exclusive interview at www.bizchix.com/RESET

"I had tried meditation so many times in the past," she told me. "And just couldn't get into it. I'm very type A. I'm a huge overachiever. I felt I wasn't good at meditation, so I shouldn't spend my time on it. If I can't get the A+ on meditation, why [do] it?"

After deciding she could commit to four minutes every day, Danielle looked through the book and found one quick meditation that spoke to her. She put it into action. The result?

"Meditation brought about a notable difference in my day." A few of my clients and friends also use the app Headspace to help their meditation journey.

How to Get Started

Need an extra nudge? Here are a few ways to start integrating gratitude into your life.

- Buy a gratitude journal, or grab a spare notebook in your house. Write in it once a day.
- Write one thing you're grateful for in dry-erase marker on your mirror every day.
- Tell one person you're grateful for them each day.
- Say, *I am grateful for my business*, out loud before starting work each day.
- Tell your partner or a friend at least one win you had today.
- Use the space provided at the end of this chapter to write three things you're grateful for.

Now go. Take some gratitude action.

Go Take Some Action!

Write 3 things you are grateful for.

1.

2.

3.

Chapter 16
Growth Mindset

> "The passion for stretching yourself and sticking to it, even (or especially) when it's not going well, is the hallmark of the growth mindset."
>
> —Carol S. Dweck, psychologist and leading researcher in the field of motivation

Meet Amber Hawley[†]

Amber is a Licensed Marriage and Family Therapist who has an MS in Counseling Psychology and a thriving group therapy practice in Silicon Valley. Her specialty is with high-achieving couples. This isn't even her first career—she used to do corporate taxes before this.

As part of my work in preparing for this book, Amber and I sat down to discuss her experience working with high achievers and their mindset. What she taught me about the growth mindset was very powerful. First, let's start with Amber's favorite leader on the subject.

Growth vs. Fixed Mindset

Carol S. Dweck Ph.D. is a psychologist best known for her best-selling book *Mindset*.[36] This classic piece of literature has been key in helping anyone—not just entrepreneurs—change their life and, you guessed it, their mindset.

Dweck's prestigious career started with a fascination over how people coped with failure. Over the course of thirty years, her research spawned a whole new paradigm.

[†] Interested in connecting for in-person or virtual work with Amber? Visit amberhawley.com.

> "My research has shown that the view you adopt for yourself profoundly affects the way you lead your life."
> —*Carol S. Dweck*

In *Mindset*, Dweck sets out two mindsets that she found through her work with people of all ages (yes, even children): Growth and Fixed.

In a fixed mindset, you believe that what you have is all you'll have; you can't be smarter, change your personality, or control the way things pan out. People with a fixed mindset tend to feel that they have to prove themselves over and over again, require constant validation, or have an unhealthy level of codependency. In this mindset, people tend to see criticism or feedback as pointing out a character flaw, not as an opportunity for improvement. Setbacks can be debilitating.

In a growth mindset, everything you have is just a starting point and can be expanded upon. People with a growth mindset believe you can influence your own life through effort, help from others, and the way you approach things. They do not believe that who they are, or what they can do, is cemented. Growth oriented individuals tend to believe that external things don't define them; they work hard, don't shirk from failure, and keep going. Setbacks are just another time to learn and move forward again.

Yes, you can be both. In fact, it is a spectrum that you ebb and flow on.

You can have a fixed mindset in one area of your life, and a very healthy growth mindset in another. This is not straight across the board or even cut-and-dry. It can be fluid. And believe it or not, these mindsets are found in children. Many school districts are instructing children and parents on fixed and growth mindsets.

In fact, Dweck's research into mindset—and subsequent discovery of these two mindsets—was started because of an experiment she conducted with young children.

Childhood Mindsets

You may have grown up in a home with parents who had predominantly fixed mindsets. Perhaps that influenced the way you saw yourself then ... and the way you see yourself now.

Are you making business decisions based on a fixed mindset? Do you know that failing to get that speech, client, product, or service is one more opportunity to learn? Are you in a growth-oriented mindset about client acquisition, but a fixed mindset about money?

Can you unwind these tendrils and see where it all started for you?

Part of coping with our childhood, and the mindset issues that stemmed from it, will come back to asking yourself these questions: do I have a fixed mindset or a growth mindset about this issue?

And why?

It's a powerful exploration of the foundation that stands beneath us. We're standing on the experiences of our childhood, but sometimes, we still don't even know what's down there.

As a coach, I see clients and colleagues get stuck in a problem for a long time. Two entrepreneurs with the same business and the same skill set go through the same problem, except one works through the issue quickly, and one slowly, or even remains stuck. It's like the turtle and the hare. The hare doesn't go into the pit of depression or watch Netflix for a month.

The difference is a fixed versus growth mindset.

Changing Your Mindset

You absolutely can change your mindset from fixed to growth. Guess what? It comes back to R.E.S.E.T.-ing your thoughts.

> **R—Recognize** that you're in a fixed mindset.
>
> **E—Evaluate** why you feel you cannot change, or cannot learn, or cannot grow. Is there something behind that? Is the problem externally oriented or internally oriented? Do you feel like your locus of control is within you, or do you feel like everything is determined by external factors?
>
> **S—Stories** you are telling yourself about your mindset? Can you "what if?" yourself into the worst-case scenario?
>
> **E—Enough** time has passed in a fixed mindset. Decide to switch to a growth mindset.
>
> Now let's **T—Take** some action.

Amber gave me several amazing action steps for how to move from a fixed mindset into a growth mindset.

1. Expose yourself to new ideas and new ways of thinking.
2. Learn how to take feedback without hating yourself. Gather data and analyze it. (Let's face it—you're doing all that right now just by reading this book.)
3. Author and life coach Tony Robbins says, *you can be upset about something for 90 seconds, and then move on.* Of course, maybe you're not there yet. You might need a day to wallow and evolve. Instead of a whole week, resolve to only wallow for an hour.
4. Sing the tune of leadership guru Jim Rohn: "Don't wish it was easier; wish you were better."
5. Give yourself permission to have self-care time.
6. Focus on progress over perfection. Let's say something happens that, in your fixed mindset, feels like the worst thing ever. You have a low month of sales or you lost a client. You immediately go to the place of *I'm not good at this. Things aren't working, etc.* Then, you recognize that you're taking that out of your worth. Even if nothing else changes—you still wallow, you withdraw, whatever—it's still a win! You recognized what you were doing and saying in your mind. That's the first step to change, and that's progress. People with a fixed mindset never get here.

For Those in a Dark Place

Right now you might be saying to yourself: *This is nice, but you don't know what I've been through. Where is the hope for me?*

First of all, I've been in a really dark place before too, and I want you to know there is hope for you.

Yes. You.

The point of this chapter is to remember that your life situation and your mindset are not fixed. You are not stuck. Everything is changeable. You have the ability to change your life, but some things are just really hard. If it doesn't come easy, it's not because you're destined to be a failure. These things were probably set up at a young age and have a solid hold.

"You can know something intellectually," Amber told me, "but not really feel it in your heart."

Give it time to sink into your heart.

It may take you longer because of the situation you're in or dealing with, but that's okay. Focus on the progress you're making, even if it's incremental. Remember that you're at A right now, and you want to get to Z. But you don't go right to Z. You have to hit B, C, maybe you can skip D, but you still have other letters you have to get through.

You will get there. And if you feel like you are stuck and can't get there on your own, throw up a white flag and ask for help. Reach out to a friend, mentor, coach, or therapist. I cannot tell you how life-changing therapy has been for me.

Resiliency

This isn't easy, right?

Even people that have a growth mindset—or have the gift of being raised in an environment with a growth mindset—will hit criticism. It will hurt. You're going to mess up. You're human.

The key is resiliency.

Say to yourself, *I'm going to have these wounds, lick them, have my moment, but I'm going to bounce back quicker.*

Let's go back to Karen DeYoung for a moment. Karen was definitely raised with a growth mindset, but she didn't even realize it.

Both her parents were federal workers with the United States government and had steady, 9-5 jobs their entire careers. They, however, grew up in the era of segregation. Karen grew up on stories about them walking past the white school to get to the black school where the books and facilities were sub-par. And how they couldn't go into certain restaurants.

Yet, they never spoke about their experience with a *woe is me* attitude.

Her parents never took on a victim role. They had hope for a better future for themselves and their children. Because of this and a lot of hard work, they accomplished a lot. They never spoke of their experience in the negative because they were always focused on how they could better themselves. They had gratitude for their jobs, which were steady. In these ways, they really instilled resiliency in their children.

It's a stunning example of a can-do attitude.

Imagine how many people get stuck in a horrible, negative situation and don't believe they can do different, have better, or be better?

You Are Here

All the ladies featured in this book have a growth mindset. They are constantly looking to learn and grow, and are willing to transform themselves. Guess what?

So do you.

If you are reading this, you have a growth mindset. If you had a fixed mindset, you wouldn't believe that this, or any book, would help you, so you wouldn't have even picked this up. Great work! You've arrived ready for change.

As you go forward with improving your mindset and striving for more, I want you to keep one more thing in mind: Not everybody in your life is going to have a growth mindset or even understand your need to develop one.

You may be married to someone with a fixed mindset that doesn't desire change. Your family or friends may feel uncomfortable when you shift your mindset and strive for better. That's normal. Not happy, necessarily, but normal.

Protect yourself.

Surround yourself with people who are growing, striving, cultivating awareness, and always seeking higher. Women like that are part of the reason why I love working with female entrepreneurs.

If you need a place to find them? Come hang out with the rest of the BizChix[†] on Facebook. We have your back. We'll be your growth cheerleaders.

---

† Visit us there at www.bizchix.com/join

Chapter 17
R.E.S.E.T. Again and Again

> "Mindset is never one and done."
> —*Natalie Eckdahl*

I want to reiterate something very important: Mindset isn't something that you complete once and walk away from. You're going to have to R.E.S.E.T. many, many times.

This book isn't something you check off your list and congratulate yourself for having accomplished reading it. Think of it as a resource for you to come back to each time you need support with mindset issues. I want you to be proud of yourself for seeking better, finding new information, and exposing yourself to new ideas.

It takes great courage to be an entrepreneur and it takes great courage to face our mindset issues.

Don't let mindset issues or your current life situation keep you from becoming the woman you were meant to be.

The Natalie of fifteen years ago could not have dreamed up this life or this business. I was in a dark and broken place. The life I planned out for myself and my family had been shattered. I didn't have the tools to work through the grief, let alone see a different future.

Can you believe how far I've come?

If you are in a broken place, please give yourself the gift of time to process your hurt and grief—preferably with a qualified professional. The passage of time heals so much. Investing time and money to work through my grief, anger, sadness, and deep pain was worth it. I'm so grateful to my therapists who sat with me during these pivotal moments. (Thank you Carol, Barbara and Jeff for all you did for me.)

I share my personal story of betrayal and a failed marriage not for sympathy or for you to hate my ex. (I don't!) I want to give you hope.

And I want to share a surprising revelation: I would not change any of it.

My healing was a process that took me through a path of introspection and self development. I'm a better mother, friend, and daughter. I also attracted a healthier and more supportive man who partners with me in all areas, loves my daughter with all his heart, and with whom I gave life to two amazing boys. Our marriage is not perfect by any means, but is filled with honesty, trust, and love.

Because of my ex's affair and the end of our marriage, I'm more empathetic to others pain. I've discovered the deep power of my intuition. And all of this has led to where I am now: coaching and impacting women on a global scale.

I wouldn't be the woman or coach I am today without all of my experiences.

As you finish this book, you'll want your mindset issues to resolve immediately. Continually remind yourself that mindset is a process and a journey. I know you. I see you. I know you're used to achieving and conquering, but this is different from a to-do list. You will continually work on your mindset as you reach new heights in business and leadership. New mindset issues will crop up. Those old favorites will resurface.

That's okay.

You won't be stuck for long if you keep using the R.E.S.E.T. Framework. When you notice that you're having a new mindset issue, this book will be here. The long form video interviews of the women featured in this book will encourage you. (I highly recommend you watch them at www.bizchix.com).

I will still be here.

Connect with me through my podcasts, my website, Instagram, my live events, or email me at natalie@bizchix.com. (Really.) I'd love to know how you are R.E.S.E.T.-ing your mindset and I'd be honored if you would tell a friend (or a hundred!) about this book.

Remember, you are not alone. I believe in you.

Now go, take some action.

About the Author

Natalie Eckdahl is a Business Strategist and High Performance Coach who helps high-achieving women entrepreneurs build, grow, and scale their businesses while avoiding overwhelm.

She's the founder of the BizChix Community, Podcast, Programs, and Events and has been recognized as "One of the Top Women in Business to Listen to." She has also been featured in Inc, Fast Company, Huffington Post, and Entrepreneur.

Natalie brings a multidisciplinary perspective to her work. She draws from her MBA education, 20+ years of work experience, deep intuition, and over 250 podcast interviews with industry influencers to help her clients with customized strategy and coaching to reach 6 figures+ in profits.

She currently lives in California with her husband and three children.

Connect with Natalie:
Instagram—@bizchixpodcast
#RESETmindsetbook

References

Chapter 2
1   Gallwey, W. Timothy. The Inner Game of Tennis. London: Pan Books, 1975.

2   Drake Baer, "One of America's most beloved authors just told us her 'number one life hack' for lasting relationships," Business Insider, August 26, 2016, http://www.businessinsider.com/brene-browns-biggest-life-hack-is-a-simple-phrase-2015-8#ixzz3jvxF2qfw.

3   Brown, Brené. Rising Strong. (New York: Spiegel & Grau, an imprint of Random House. 2015).

4   Slovic, Paul. "The Psychology of Protective Behavior." 1978. Journal of Safety Research, 10(2), 58-68. http://hdl.handle.net/1794/22386.

Chapter 4
5   Ed Diener and Martin E.P. Seligman, "Very Happy People," Psychological Science, 13 no 1 (2002): 81-84, https://doi.org/10.1111/1467-9280.00415.

6   M. E. P Seligman, "Positive Psychology, Positive Prevention, and Positive Therapy," In C. R. Snyder & S. J. Lopez (Eds.), Handbook of Positive Psychology (2002), pp. 3-9, New York, NY, US: Oxford University Press.

7   Landsbaum, Claire. "Mindy Kaling Gave Pixar's Inside Out It's Bittersweet Slogan." Vulture. May 30, 2015. Accessed August 11, 2018. http://www.vulture.com/2015/05/mindy-kaling-gave-inside-out-its-slogan.html.

8   Felitti, V. J., Anda, R. F., Nordenberg, D., Williamson, D. F., Spitz, A. M., Edwards, V., Marks, J. S. (1998). "Relationship of childhood abuse and household dysfunction to many of the leading causes of death in adults: The Adverse Childhood Experiences (ACE) Study," American Journal of Preventive Medicine, 14, no. 4, 245-258. http://dx.doi.org/10.1016/S0749-3797(98)00017-8.

9   De Waal, F. (1999). "The End of Nature Versus Nurture," Scientific American, 281 no. 6, 94-99. Retrieved from http://www.jstor.org/stable/26058526

10 Dweck, Carol S., Mindset: The New Psychology of Success (New York: Ballantine Books, 2008), 5-6.

Chapter 5
11 Samantha Simon, "25 Stars Who Suffer From Imposter Syndrome," InStyle, 2017, https://www.instyle.com/celebrity/stars-imposter-syndrome.

Chapter 6

12 Paul L. Hewitt, and Gordon L. Flett, "Dimensions of Perfectionism in Unipolar Depression," Journal of Abnormal Psychology, 100, no. 1, (February 1991): 98-101, http://psycnet.apa.org/buy/1991-18565-001.

13 Paul L. Hewitt, Gordon L. Flett, and Evelyn Ediger, "Perfectionism Traits and Perfectionistic Self-Presentation in Eating Disorder Attitudes, Characteristics, and Symptoms," International Journal of Eating Disorders, 18, no. 4, (1995): 317-326.

14 Randy O. Frost, and Gail Steketee, "Perfectionism in Obsessive-Compulsive Disorder Patients," Behaviour Research and Therapy, 35, no. 4 (April 1997): 291-296, https://doi.org/10.1016/S0005-7967(96)00108-8.

15 K.G. Rice, C.M.E. Richardson, and D. Clark, "Perfectionism, Procrastination, and Psychological Distress," Journal of Counseling Psychology, 59, no. 2 (2012): 288-302. http://dx.doi.org/10.1037/a0026643.

16 11, 2010 June. "Fear of Shipping." Seth's Blog. June 11, 2010. Accessed August 11, 2018. https://seths.blog/2010/06/fear-of-shipping/.

17 LeDoux, J. Cell Mol Neurobiol (2003) 23: 727. https://doi.org/10.1023/A:1025048802629.

18 Naim, Rania. "30 Iconic Quotes To Help You Overcome The Fear Of Failure." Thought Catalog. April 22, 2016. Accessed August 11, 2018. https://thoughtcatalog.com/rania-naim/2016/04/30-iconic-quotes-to-help-you-overcome-the-fear-of-failure/.

Chapter 8

19 "What Judging Others Reveals About You." The Positivity Solution. Accessed August 11, 2018. http://thepositivitysolution.com/judging-others/.

20 Winfrey, Oprah. "Reese Witherspoon and Mindy Kaling: Brave New Worlds." Oprah SuperSoul Conversations. Podcast audio, February 13, 2018. https://www.youtube.com/watch?v=UgD4X_q3euA

Chapter 9

21 Karen D. Multon, Steven D. Brown, and Robert W. Lent, "Relation of self-efficacy beliefs to academic outcomes: A meta-analytic investigation," Journal of Counseling Psychology, 38, no. 1, (January 1991): 30-38.

22 L. DiAnne Borders, and Kathleen A. Archadel, "Self-Beliefs and Career Counseling," Journal of Career Development, 14, no. 2 (December 1, 1987): 69-79, https://doi.org/10.1177/089484538701400201.

23 "Jim Rohn Biography » Jim Rohn Blog." Jim Rohn Blog. Accessed August 11, 2018. https://www.jimrohn.com/jim-rohn-biography/.

Chapter 10

24 Orman, Suze. The 9 Steps to Financial Freedom. New York: Crown Publishers, 2001.

Chapter 11

25 Peter Salmon, "Effects of physical exercise on anxiety, depression, and sensitivity to stress: A unifying theory," Clinical Psychology Review, 21, no. 1, (February, 2001): 33-61, https://doi.org/10.1016/S0272-7358(99)00032-X

Chapter 12

26 Rosener, Judy B. "Ways Women Lead." Leadership, Gender, and Organization Issues in Business Ethics, November 1, 1990, 19-29. Accessed September 8, 2018. doi:10.1007/978-90-481-9014-0_3.

Chapter 13

27 Cohn, Michael A., Barbara L. Fredrickson, Stephanie L. Brown, Joseph A. Mikels, and Anne M. Conway. "Happiness Unpacked: Positive Emotions Increase Life Satisfaction by Building Resilience." Emotion9, no. 3 (June 2009): 361-68. Accessed September 9, 2018. doi:10.1037/a0015952.

28 Oettingen, Gabriele, and Thomas A. Wadden. "Expectation, Fantasy, and Weight Loss: Is the Impact of Positive Thinking Always Positive?" Cognitive Therapy and Research15, no. 2 (April 1991): 167-75. Accessed September 9, 2018. doi:10.1007/bf01173206.

29 Macleod, Andrew K., and Richard Moore. "Positive Thinking Revisited: Positive Cognitions, Well-being and Mental Health." Clinical Psychology & Psychotherapy7, no. 1 (2000): 1-10. Accessed September 9, 2018. doi:10.1002/(sici)1099-0879(200002)7:13.0.co;2-s.

Chapter 14

30 Maltz, Maxwell. Psycho-cybernetics. New York: TarcherPerigee, an Imprint of Penguin Books, 2016.

31 "What Oprah Learned from Jim Carrey." Oprah.com. October 12, 2011. Accessed September 09, 2018. http://www.oprah.com/oprahs-lifeclass/What-Oprah-Learned-from-Jim-Carrey-Video.

32 Gervais, Michael., and Honnold, Alex. "Using Imagery to Train for El Capitan." Finding Mastery. March 30, 2018. Accessed September 09, 2018. https://findingmastery.net/using-imagery-to-train-for-el-capitan/.

33 Gallo, Carmine. "3 Daily Habits Of Peak Performers, According To Michael Phelps' Coach." Forbes. August 08, 2016. Accessed September 09, 2018. https://www.forbes.com/sites/carminegallo/2016/05/24/3-daily-habits-of-peak-performers-according-to-michael-phelps-coach/.

34 Ito, Tiffany A., Jeff T. Larsen, N. Kyle Smith, and John T. Cacioppo. "Negative Information Weighs More Heavily on the Brain: The Negativity Bias in Evaluative Categorizations." Journal of Personality and Social Psychology75, no. 4 (October 1998): 887-900. Accessed September 9, 2018. doi:10.1037/0022-3514.75.4.887.

Chapter 15

35 Borucki, Rebekah. You Have 4 Minutes to Change Your Life: Simple 4-minute Meditations for Inspiration, Transformation, and True Bliss. Carlsbad, CA: Hay House, 2017.

Chapter 16

36 Dweck, Carol S. Mindset: The New Psychology of Success: How We Can Learn to Fulfill Our Potential: Parenting, Business, School, Relationships. New York: Ballentine Books, 2016.

Other works I consulted while writing this book:

Effects of Our Childhood: Miller, Alice. The Drama of the Gifted Child: The Search for the True Self. New York: BasicBooks, 2008.

Meditation: Borucki, Rebekah. You Have 4 Minutes to Change Your Life: Simple 4-minute Meditations for Inspiration, Transformation, and True Bliss. Carlsbad, CA: Hay House, 2017.

Mindset: Brown, Brené. Rising Strong How the Ability to Reset Transforms the Way We Live, Love, Parent, and Lead. Random House, 2017.

Money Mindset: Sincero, Jen. You Are a Badass at Making Money: Master the Mindset of Wealth. New York: Penguin Books, an Imprint of Penguin Random House LLC, 2018.

Overcoming Doubt and Insecurity: Gallwey, W. Timothy. The Inner Game of Tennis. London: Pan Books, 1975.

Perfectionism: Brown, Brené. The Gifts of Imperfection: Let Go of Who You Think You're Supposed to Be and Embrace Who You Are. Center City, MN: Hazelden, 2010.

Taking Action: Brown, Brené. Daring Greatly: How the Courage to Be Vulnerable Transforms the Way We Live, Love, Parent, and Lead. London, England: Penguin Books, 2015.

Taking Action: Olson, Jeff. The Slight Edge: Turning Simple Disciplines into Massive Success and Happiness. McMahons Point, Sydney Australia: Goko Publishing, 2016.

Taking Action: Robbins, Mel. The 5 Second Rule: Transform Your Life, Work, and Confidence with Everyday Courage. United States of America: Savio Republic, 2017.

Made in the USA
San Bernardino, CA
18 October 2018